BROADCAST NEWSWRITING AS PROCESS

Developed under the
advisory editorship of
Thomas W. Bohn, Dean,
School of Communications,
Ithaca College

BROADCAST NEWSWRITING AS PROCESS

J. Clark Weaver

COLLEGE OF COMMUNICATIONS
FLORIDA STATE UNIVERSITY

Longman

New York & London

BROADCAST NEWSWRITING AS PROCESS

Longman Inc., 1560 Broadway, New York, N.Y. 10036
Associated companies, branches, and representatives
throughout the world.

Developmental Editor: Gordon Anderson
Editorial and Design Supervisor: Harriet Sigerman
Production Supervisor: Ferne Kawahara
Manufacturing Supervisor: Marion Hess

Library of Congress Cataloging in Publication Data

Weaver, J. Clark.
  Broadcast newswriting as process.

  Includes bibliographical references and index.
  1. Broadcast journalism—Authorship. I. Title.
PN4784.B75W4   1984   808'.06607   83-9901
ISBN 0-582-28453-8 (pbk.)

Permission to reprint "The Elephant Child" from *Just So Stories*
by Rudyard Kipling on p. 40 was granted by Doubleday & Company,
New York, New York and A. P. Watt Ltd., Literary Agents, London.

Permission to reprint the broadcast script on pp. 72–73 was granted
by Caralyn Jones on Channel 12, WTLV, Jacksonville, Florida.

Manufactured in the United States of America
Printing: 9 8 7 6 5 4 3 2 1   Year: 92 91 90 89 88 87 86 85 84

Contents

v

Preface

Many young people want a career in broadcast newswriting. But many of those applying for jobs report the same problem. Without experience they get no job. Without a job they get no experience. However, even without experience, many report they have no problem when their portfolios indicate, or they personally demonstrate, that they can write.

The need for broadcast writers is well known. *Broadcasting* magazine has long observed that the top skill demand in the industry is the ability to develop ideas and express feelings on paper. It would, therefore, seem that being able to perform skillfully as a writer is the key that unlocks the door to a broadcast news career.

This textbook has been developed around procedures essential to acquiring an efficient and effective writing ability for radio and television news. As a result, it is concerned primarily with *how* to write. And because writers do need expertise in more than one type of newswriting, it is also concerned with the writing of the commentary, analysis, editorial, review, and interview. All of these are prerequisite experiences to that growing field—investigative reporting.

For years most of us who teach newswriting assumed that being able to write came built in, an exclusive product of talent. This concept implies that either you can write or you can't. However, recent experiences in teaching radio and television newswriting indicate that, given the desire, how to write can be learned.

The basic concept of this text is that newswriting can be learned, just as can driving a car or swimming, when the learning effort is changed from trial and error and organized around a *process*. Learning newswriting by following a specific procedure is possible because the process approach in this text is heuristic. Each process and its steps helps you develop the necessary writing skills. As a result the process approach maximizes your learning.

Maximization of learning is possible because each process in this text enables you to combine writing with technique and theory. Therefore, as a beginning broadcast newswriter you benefit in two ways: (1) you develop a comprehensive understanding of broadcast newswriting, and (2) you acquire specific writing skills and techniques essential to successful newswriting.

For example, Chapter 1 helps you conceptualize what is involved in newswriting. Chapter 2 gives you techniques that successful reporters use in identifying and recognizing news and its significance. This chapter also helps you distinguish between radio and television newswriting. Chapter 3 helps you attain the specific procedures that are essential to developing a newswriting style. Chapter 4 takes you through the procedures essential to writing news. You gather information, develop a fact sheet, write leads, and then with the help of the processes you learn how to write hard news, soft news, and dramatic news. Each *process* has a number of different steps to assure adequate development of a news subject through writing techniques.

Naturally you should become proficient in using each step in each process because doing so will develop your writing capability. It is in this way that each process moves your writing ability forward.

The *processes* in Chapter 4 also help you develop a feeling about writing. This is important because, as is well known, no two people develop writing skills at the same rate or to the same degree in the same period of time. This is inevitable because no two people have identical physiological, neurological, neurological, or psychological profiles.

Chapters 5 and 6 are concerned with the mechanics of writing. Not every writer will need to spend a lot of time with these details. However, information about words and their use in writing is similar to having some understanding of what's under the hood of the car you drive. For example, in newswriting, the misuse of words, like a disconnected spark plug wire, can impede forward progress. And because language is an essential in the newswriting craft, knowing how to remedy word problems expedites progress in learning how to write. Other procedures for triumphing over writing problems are included in these two chapters on the assumption that learning to write radio and television news will give you a feeling of accomplishment.

Writing news can be a fulfilling accomplishment because doing so is one of the more satisfying ways to experience the world in which we live. Furthermore, most broadcast newswriters sooner or later discover that writing news means being an active part of a culture that adds fullness to their lives.

Chapter 7 assumes that you will have acquired certain writing skills and techniques. This chapter is concerned with writing the commentary, analysis, editorial, review, and the interview. In this chapter you will see that excellence in communicating does not just happen. It is made to happen. And helping the writer discover *how* to make it happen is the basic purpose of the processes in this text.

To paraphrase Alfred North Whitehead,* the use of a process in learning to write news helps one take an idea and relate it to the human stream of sense perceptions, feelings, hopes, and desires found in all mental and emotional activities. And that is the stuff of which good broadcast newswriting is made.

It is a fact of experience that the more disciplined your writing is the sooner you will write *intuitively*. To help my students achieve this state, I ask each one to write fifty or more assignments during an academic term. This number does not include the rewrites. Neither do the students receive a grade until the last two weeks. Up to that time each receives an "O.K." or a "Rewrite" with specific reference to text passages that will promote improvement.

And they tell me from their first jobs that although they may not have believed that so much writing was that important at the time, they now know it was worth it. One student wrote from her first network TV-outlet news job, "They forgot to tell me I was not to do my own standup the first time out. I broke a station precedent. But they said it was okay because I can write."

Incidentally, the majority of the established network writers are print-media trained. As a result of this fact many executives responsible for hiring newswriters tend to believe that getting print-media writing experience before turning to radio and television is essential to success in broadcast newswriting. Furthermore, they cite as evidence such names and personalities as David Brinkley, John Chancellor, Walter Cronkite, Harry Reasoner, Mike Wallace, and many others.

The list is impressive because each one is a superior writer. But the background is that these top writers for the networks are accidents of a new industry. True, each person was print-media trained. But each was ambitious, and radio and television were maverick industries. Furthermore, the available source from which writers could be hired was the print media.

Now that these former "eye-media" writers are successfully doing "ear-media" writing, it is only natural that some of both radio and television management should continue to deduce that print-media training is the best preparation for a career in broadcast newswriting. Even some of these writers are advocates of this procedure.

This sort of coincidence has always dominated human thinking. There are thousands of such misconceptions in socioeconomic cultural history. We are consistently trying to progress by taking what we know and expecting it to solve the problems of the unknown. That is why it took us so long to learn to fly. That is also why leeches and bloodletting,

---

* Alfred North Whitehead, *The Aims of Education*, (New York: Macmillan Co., 1957), pp. 15–31.

not too long ago (and unfortunately for the lives of many), were used as medical techniques to treat human ailments.

However, it is reasonable to assume that in time, now that broadcast communication is producing newswriters, the most readily available and adequately experienced writers will be those who develop their skills without the double duty of having to transpose one style of writing into another. When that time comes, and many believe it is now here, the broadcast newswriter will truly be a specialist, not a born again print-media newswriter whose genius assures success.

When you do apply for a newswriting job, be sure to take with you a portfolio of news stories you have written. Also be prepared to offer to demonstrate your ability on the spot. If you know how to write you will also be able to adjust to the specific routines you find at that station. Being able to adjust to new circumstances is the nature of living and writing in the broadcast world.

This text, *Broadcast Newswriting as a Process*, is a product of all that I, as a teacher and writer, have read and all that I have come to know. Included in my reading is the work of some who were around when recorded history began. Other names on that list are legion. Their writings extend from pre-Aristotelian times to the present.

I am indebted to them all because what they wrote kept me busy reading dramas, poetry, narratives, history, literature, mathematics, philosophy, geography, archeology, sociology, science, geology, psychology, psychiatry, and humor. The sources were books, magazines, research papers, and journals. And because all of what I read became so much a part of me, it is doubtful that the subject matter presented in this book can be said to be my own.

I'm also sure that much of what I say about writing broadcast news is a partial answer to students who years ago, in spite of my teaching expertise, were unable to write but could ask disturbing questions about why not. Most of what they wanted to know took years to answer. And the replies, I do believe, are in the *process*. At least the students today who use them to develop their writing skills do a better job. Furthermore, most of them today learn how to write sooner and much better than their talent, their intuition, and their ability at first indicated.

Suggestions in this text are, in part, based on letters received from former students who told me how they became performers, speechwriters, actors, politicians, barkeeps, Ph.Ds, judges, TV and movie directors, priests, lawyers, teachers, housewives, mothers, and loyal alumni. I appreciate all their contributions and thank them for their help.

For feedback and contributions to the concepts in this text, my special thanks to Thomas W. Bohn, Dean, School of Communications, Ithaca College; Theodore Clevenger, Jr., Dean, College of Communication, Florida State University; Dr. Mickie N. Edwardson, College of Journalism and Communication, University of Florida; Dr. Douglas P. Starr, Department of Journalism, North Texas State University; Howard Kelley, News Director, WTLV Channel 12, Jacksonville, Florida; Executive Editor Gordon T. R. Anderson; Editorial Assistant Veta J. Maillard; Editorial and Design Supervisor Harriet Sigerman; and especially to Inez K. at home.

J. Clark Weaver

CHAPTER 1

The Oral-Aural Communication Theory

THE BASIC CONCEPT

The concept that oral-aural communication is a process was first advanced by two mathematicians, Claude E. Shannon and Warren Weaver. Weaver developed the oral-aural aspect of the theory after Shannon developed a signal process that improved electronic channeling from a specific *source* to a specific *receiver*. The explanation and development of this theory as it parallels oral-aural communication was published in 1949 by the University of Illinois Press under the title *The Mathematical Theory of Communication*. Since that time the Shannon-Weaver communication theory has been researched, diagrammed, and described in many ways. The concept has also been adjusted and adapted to include all forms of communication.

As everyone knows, person-to-person communication is a two-way process. Someone talks, or signals, and someone hears, or sees, what is being signaled. Then the person hearing and seeing reacts in response to the person who is the source of the message.

All human communication is a process whether it is an audible signal, a visible signal, or a combination of the two. Person-to-person communicating includes the following: there is the source, the person who is initiating the *message*; the *message*, that which is being said or signaled by the source; the *channel*, the source's voice, signs, or both; and the *receiver*, the person who is hearing the vocal sounds or seeing the signs that comprise the message.

ENCODING, DECODING, FEEDBACK

Three additional steps are needed to fulfill the function of this process. These three steps are especially important to the newswriter because accurate use of them is essential to successful reporting.

1. *Encoding*. Before the communication of a news story can begin, the information from which it is to be developed must be collected and organized. Following this procedure, the act of writing the message, the news story, is referred to as encoding. Encoding a news story is the newswriter's special responsibility.

2. *Decoding*. This step involves the receiver's (the listener-viewer's) interpretation of the message, the news story. Decoding as a step in the communication process is fundamental to the listener-viewer's response. The receiver's response as a result of decoding a message is called feedback.

3. *Feedback*. Feedback is the receiver's reaction to the message. In conversation the receiver's feedback is generally directed toward the source and is a reaction to what that person is saying or has said. Feedback during conversation is directed toward the source in direct ratio to the degree of congruity and incongruity a receiver recognizes in the message. For example:

> FIFTEEN-YEAR-OLD: "I want the car tonight. I have a date."
> PARENT: "You cannot have the car until after you are sixteen and are a licensed driver."

In newswriting it is the responsibility of the source to encode so that the information about an event that may happen, is happening, or has happened will generate congruous satisfaction that accompanies understanding.

Advocacy and Feedback

There is one aspect of newswriting that should never be allowed to get in the way of satisfactory feedback. Advocacy reporting implies that the writer is taking sides. What the reporter writes is therefore likely to be a value judgment, a personal point of view. This places the writer in a position of being either for what is being reported or against it. The receiver may feel that the source (the writer) is either right or wrong, or is making either a good or a bad judgment. When this reaction takes place the feedback may be directed specifically toward the source.

Specificity and Feedback

The role of an efficient broadcast newswriter is to report the facts. Being specific is necessary to avoid developing or creating misunderstanding between the listener-viewer and the newswriter.

Specificity in the literal sense of that word should never be used. When the writer literally adheres to specificity, an additional problem is created. Pure specificity has little meaning. For example:

BIRDS SING. BOY PLAYS. CAR WRECKED.

Pure specificity is barren writing.

Generality and Feedback

The opposite of specificity is generality. Generality is writing that has few facts. Therefore, generality as a writing technique means that the writer talks too much and says too little.

HOW TO CONTROL FEEDBACK

Communicate Accurately

The newswriter who would learn to communicate accurately and help control feedback needs to strike a happy medium between the two extremes of specificity and generality. By so doing the writer will develop an ability to create optimum specificity and optimum generality. While the degree of how much of each should be used can never be defined by rule, an adequate overlap of these two aspects will help each part of a news story relate to every other part and in so doing help the listener-viewer, the receiver, better understand the encoder's message, the news story. Because of this, understanding the feedback will comply with the intention of all well-written news stories.

Understanding the Receiver's Frame of Reference

The newswriter also needs to develop a special understanding of the receiver. One way that you, the source, can increase your understanding is to become aware of the frames of reference that most often interfere with the receiver's decoding. These primary frames of reference involve the listener-viewer's attitudes toward family, neighbors, job, age, race, health, occupation, income, social values, beliefs, religion, and other aspects of an environment that may engender personal stress as it relates to reactions and attitudes.

Personal stress of some kind generally accompanies all our efforts. That is why encoding may be a special problem for the source, just as personal stress may interfere with the receiver's decoding. The source and the receiver are both human beings and each one may have personality dominances that on occasion get in the way of being objective. When this occurs, feelings and concepts about *self* as it relates to society, government, religion, and life in general may interfere with objectivity and sound judgment.

Another way for the newswriter to become objective about encoding is to try visualizing all the possible frames of reference known to the listener-viewers who will be hearing the news story. While doing this, you, the writer, should remember that each listener-viewer or receiver may have a dominant personality frame of reference that may disrupt his or her objective decoding efforts. The listener-viewer's frame of reference may exist because the receiver is socially shy, lacking in skills, feeling insecure, lacking in confidence, having a headache, is introverted, lacking in drive, dominated by someone, dependent on someone, lacking in verbal skills, domineering, indecisive, nervous, unhappy, unrealistic, intelligent, self-conscious, aggressive, belligerent, extroverted, generous, rationalizing, cheerful, unstable, self-seeking, aloof, retiring, sexually aggressive, anxious, practical, purposeful, dominated by a sense of power, or feels in need of friends, feels slighted, is unaware of a sense of purpose, and hundreds of other personality dominances that are related to self concepts.

In addition to understanding how these personality dominances influence both encoding and decoding, the radio and/or television newswriter should also keep in mind how the many confusing and distracting aspects of an environment may also interfere with receiver decoding of a news message. For example, the listener-viewer may be distracted during the newscast encoding because the music next door is too loud, a dog is barking, children are running, yelling, or screaming, he or she is hungry, a phone is ringing, a jet plane is flying low, a timer in the kitchen is ringing, someone is knocking at the back door, the radio or television signal is picking up static interference, the newscaster's voice is annoying, the volume is too high, plus hundreds of other distractions that haunt most listening and viewing environments.

As you think about these stress-producing distractions you will realize they are always present and you will begin to understand how essential it is that you, the newswriter, always think of encoding in terms of the listener-viewer's environment as well as in terms of his or her personality dominances. Because of the potential of these distractions, it is the responsibility of the newswriter to transfix the listener-viewer with a flow of information in the news story. When information flow is adequate, the story will be in focus and will satisfactorily contrast or compare with the listener-viewer's information and experience. When this occurs, decoding and adequate feedback take place.

HOW TO RECOGNIZE POSITIVE FEEDBACK

Generally speaking a newswriter does not receive "helpful" feedback from the listener-viewer. A receiver may call to complain about performance or the signal level, but the receiver is less likely to call about the news message and make suggestions that will be of specific help in encoding. There are exceptions when the source's facts are inconsistent or the news story is distorted. However, the absence of feedback to the writer is good feedback. Positive feedback is also indicated when the manager calls you in and gives you a raise or a promotion, or when you receive an offer from another station to write for it at a higher salary.

SUMMARY

It is important to understand the various steps and their order in the communication process because knowing the steps can be an asset to a newswriter's success. The sequence is: (1) You, the *source*, (2) *encode*, write, (3) a news *message*, (4) to be *channeled*, broadcast, (5) to the *receiver*, the listener-viewer, (6) who *decodes* the news story, (7) and reacts with appropriate *feedback*.

Before you begin writing a news story you need to explore fully the problems involved in encoding and in obtaining appropriate feedback from the receiver. To do this is essential because once the story is prepared and turned over to those whose responsibility it is to see that it is adequately channeled, it is then too late for the writer to have second thoughts about improving the message for the receiver.

Finally, every newswriter must become aware that communicating is a continuing process under varying circumstances and conditions. And because it is, the newswriter must accept the fact that there is no optimum focus in his personal needs as a writer, nor in the needs of those around him. In other words, there is no one way of doing a job right every time. For not only is newswriting a communication process, it is also a dynamic process. You will realize this when you begin using the various *writing processes* later on in this text. As a result of these two aspects of newswriting, you should take what you can from every communicating experience and use it if it is applicable to your next effort.

Newswriting standards are determined by human standards. That is why the changes that occur in radio and television news-broadcast writing, plus the need to make continuous adjustments to those changes, make working in the broadcast industry an exciting and vital adventure.

CHAPTER **2**

How to
Identify News

WHAT IS NEWS?

Newscasts are produced throughout each day for radio, television, and cablevision. And just as regularly, listener-viewers watch and hear these newscasts. The advertising sold on each newscast is an invaluable commodity for a broadcast service. This fact alone makes the production of news an essential part of each service's programming. In other words, broadcasting news is good business.

There is no adequate definition of news. Therefore, every writer of news must understand all the essential ingredients that go into this aspect of broadcasting. Let us begin understanding what news is by recognizing the fact that each individual's existence in society is filled with Happenings, Occurrences, Events, and Occasions: H-O-E-Os. Many H-O-E-Os take place as a result of deliberate planning and specific effort. Examples would be seeking office, conducting certain business transactions, traveling, making speeches, performing on television, and even getting married.

However, many happenings, occurrences, events, and occasions are the result of chance. Some of these chance H-O-E-Os are fires, storms, wrecks, robberies, and murders. Even chance H-O-E-Os may have been

7

a product of planning. But whether an H-O-E-O is planned or happens by chance, there still is the possibility that it will touch the lives of many people. The death of John Lennon is an example.

It is a perfectly normal human response to be interested in what transpires minute by minute in a highly organized society. The Cable News Network of the Turner Broadcasting System, Inc., was created to fulfill such a need.

There are many factors that determine the degree to which an H-O-E-O may be of interest to listener-viewers. To help understand some of these factors and the news selection process, let us call the information a reporter collects about any H-O-E-O a *result*. When a result is organized and written with the view to dissemination via a broadcast system, it becomes a *news story*. When several stories are combined for dissemination they are referred to as a *news report*, or *newscast*. This final combination of a series of results, a news report, or newscast, has been defined and illustrated in many ways. It may be a series of H-O-E-Os that has local interest only. An example of a local news story might be the erection of a stoplight at an intersection in a town that never had a stoplight before. Certainly that news is of interest to local residents.

Other H-O-E-Os have statewide interest. An example would be a request by a governor to a state legislature to increase property taxes.

Sometimes an H-O-E-O has interest for an entire region of the country. For example, the lack of adequate snow and rain during the winter in, say, New England, or in the Western states, can be responsible for an extreme area water shortage during the following summer. Since the entire area will be affected, naturally such a problem is of specific interest to anyone living in that region.

When a news story is of interest to people around the entire world, it is said to have international interest. Many such H-O-E-Os take place each day. However, the decision to turn any H-O-E-O into a news story depends on whether it possesses certain *news factors*. The general rule governing this decision is that one or more of these news factors must be present in an H-O-E-O to make it *newsworthy*. It is the presence of these news factors that a beginning writer must look for in every H-O-E-O.

HOW TO RECOGNIZE NEWS

The six basic news factors for which a writer should look are identified as *prominence, proximity, significance, timeliness, human interest*, and *conflict*.

Every beginning news writer should carry a working definition of each of these six news factors around in his head. Then when the writer is investigating an H-O-E-O with the view to developing a news report, he or she can quickly and readily determine the specific news angle and newsworthiness that may be served.

News Factor One: Prominence

Prominence as a news factor is that quality or state of conspicuousness, popularity, or recognition that is present in an H-O-E-O. When the qualities of prominence are present in a news story, the majority of listener-viewers will probably empathize with those involved. For example, when the daughter of an internationally known millionaire is kidnapped, prominence plays a primary role in the development of any news story about her.

Listener-viewers receive vicarious satisfaction from hearing about the lives of others, especially about the lives of those whom they envy or might like to emulate. The place that vicarious living plays in the lives of people has been demonstrated again and again in the press. Note the number of prominent personalities whose names make the daily newscasts. Their presence in these stories helps satisfy this human need. Also note the number of listener-viewers who empathetically live the daily life story of their favorite soap opera character. Also note the number of prominent places whose names appear in the news because there is something special about them to which people relate. Prominence, whether it refers to a place or a person, is a basic news factor.

News Factor Two: Proximity

Proximity as a news factor is that state of being or quality of an H-O-E-O that makes it near in place, time, or relationship. Proximity involves that which is close to a listener-viewer either directly or indirectly.

Any H-O-E-O that occurs in an individual's home, on his street, in his community, in his city, or in his region of the country may possess proximity. The determining feature is how much it affects those who are close to it. For example, the son or daughter of your neighbor is kidnapped, arrested, or held hostage. That happening is said to possess the factor of proximity, even though it may have occurred thousands of miles away while your neighbor was visiting another part of the world. Any H-O-E-O that is "close to home" possesses proximity for the person or persons who are directly or indirectly affected or concerned about the incident.

News Factor Three: Significance

Significance, as a news factor, is the quality or state of being important. Its importance also relates to the lives of those outside the area where the

H-O-E-O takes place. For example, a school building burns to the ground. None of the students or their parents was in the fire, but the fact that access to the building is now completely denied them is significant. The fire becomes a news factor through significance because, first, the school's records were completely destroyed; second, there is no place immediately available where the students may continue their education; third, the cause of the fire is discovered to be arson. The building was ignited by disgruntled students. The significance of this is brought home to all those living in the entire city system. Thus a school fire becomes a significant news factor in the lives of the population in that city.

News Factor Four: Timeliness

Timeliness as a news factor is the state or quality of immediacy. Timeliness is ever present in radio and television news. The timeliness of a news story may take precedence over a program being aired: "We interrupt this program to bring you . . ." For example, a member of a certain news staff on his lunch break notices that a bank is about to be robbed. He steps into a nearby phone booth and calls his station. The station immediately calls the police. The station also puts the phone booth reporter on the air. This means the station's listener-viewers receive a timely on-the-scene account of the robbery. From his vantage point, the reporter is not only able to inform the police, he is also able to describe what is happening as the police surround the area and the bank. As a result of his reporting, the robbery attempt fails, and the listener-viewers have empathetically been on the scene.

News Factor Five: Human Interest

Human interest as a news factor is the state or quality in an H-O-E-O that causes people to respond to it with sympathy, interest, and attention. In other words, when human interest is present in an H-O-E-O, the majority of listener-viewers will respond sympathetically to it.

Human interest is perhaps the most important of the six news factors, even though our interest in people changes as we become more sophisticated. For example, there was a time when a lone nude jogging on the beach would have been of human interest. There was also a time when a dog biting a postman would have been of interest. (Certainly the reverse does not create much human interest today. But a clever newswriter could make it so.)

You have probably noticed that the majority of television newscasts end with a "lift-in-interest-item." These short items are usually humorous, and the majority of them are one form or other of human interest.

Other examples of human interest are news stories about birds, babies, foibles, as well as strange places or things associated with people. Sometimes these are not humorous, but serious. Be that as it may, the one criterion that makes this factor different from all the others is that it is concerned specifically with people.

News Factor Six: Conflict

Conflict as a news factor is the state of—or the presence of—incompatibility, antagonism, or controversy. Whatever the H-O-E-O may be, conflict is present if there are opposing actions, intentions, divergent opinions, interests, ideas, incompatibilities, or antagonisms of any kind. Conflict is found in all dramatic actions. In fact, it is conflict that makes an action dramatic. Its presence takes on special significance if there is one dynamic force opposing another dynamic force. These conflicting forces may be physical, emotional, or ideational. The nature of the opposition, its timeliness, its significance, its proximity, and the prominence of its participants add to the dramatic conflict in an H-O-E-O and increase its priority as news.

Several years ago George Polti, whose famous book is no longer available outside the library, worked out an analysis of all the possible combinations of dramatic conflicts. He has 36 basic categories. These he has broken down into combinations of 334 subcategories. While becoming familiar with these is not essential to the beginning newswriter's success, knowing they are available is an excellent reference to have in any newswriter's kit. Some of these conflicts are present to a greater or lesser degree in all H-O-E-Os and are just waiting for the alert newswriter to use them. Here are a few.

- Man in conflict with the rules and regulations of society
- Women in conflict with men, and vice versa
- Minorities in conflict with the status quo
- Man in conflict with outer space
- Man in conflict with nature
- Man in conflict with his family, his relatives, or just himself
- Man in conflict with all or certain aspects of his environment

Conflict is present to a greater or lesser degree when two candidates from opposite parties run for the same office. It is present when any kind of problem must be solved.

Two opposing forces are present, and therefore a conflict exists, when you are driving fifty-five miles an hour in a forty-mile-an-hour zone, and a traffic officer stops you. Such an occurrence is a clash between the lawbreaker and the law. However, a story about your receiving a ticket for speeding may not make the newscast unless there are other factors present. When other news factors are present, then the writer may forget the dramatic conflict angle and use one or two of those.

For example, suppose the person given the ticket for speeding is a prominent individual whose name is widely known. This begins to qualify the H-O-E-O for a news story. Even so, the story may not be written about the ticket being given unless other factors are present.

Suppose, for example, the city council had been trying for a long time to enact a speed regulation to cover a particular street because drivers have been going too fast and injuries have occurred. And suppose you, the ticketed speeder, are the mayor's son. Now, the mayor was opposed to the speed regulation. Certain members of the city council accused him of being in favor of speeders, especially young offenders. The measure was passed in spite of his opposition. Then on the very first day the new law is in effect, his son is picked up for speeding and given a ticket. That incident might become significant news because of the several conflicts inherent in the situation.

LIBEL AND NEWSWRITING

While the identification of a person with any one of the six news factors—prominence, proximity, significance, timeliness, human interest, and conflict—is a technique that top reporters use in building up a fact sheet for a news story, what one can *really say* about that person may be limited. This potential limitation is why every beginning newswriter should have a working knowledge of the meaning of libel, the invasion of privacy, as well as the court rulings that limit what one may write about people.

The problem would be simple if one law were available that spelled out specific prohibitions and protections. Instead, there are many laws and these vary from state to state. Therefore, every newswriter must constantly be careful about what he puts on paper, even though the person about whom the reporter is writing is a "public official," and even though the 1964 United States Supreme Court ruling in the case of *The New York Times* v. *Sullivan* made it tougher for any public official to sue for libel.

Knowing when and what you can write about an individual is an *absolute must* because you can be sued for libel if you even innocently imply that certain individuals are dishonest; question a person's competence; or state or imply that a person has committed a crime, is mentally ill, has a social or other contagious disease, is subversive, or belongs to a disreputable organization.

The station or news outlet for which you work will have references and recommendations that will help you. Therefore, when in doubt read these sources. And until you are certain, and only a lawyer can come close to that, consult someone in authority. By so doing you can, in general, avoid making libelous statements.

You will also avoid being libelous if you do not sound derogatory or belittling in your newswriting, and if you avoid resorting to name calling or expressing a feeling of superiority over anyone, including a "public figure." Use the words and phrases that have been developed over the years specifically to protect you from accusations of libel while giving you some latitude in writing the story. These words and phrases are associated with the concept that a person is innocent until proven guilty. That is why the words alleged, accused, attempted robbery, and other phrases are widely used. These words and phrases must be used even though you can state facts. Even a fact has to be proven. And quoting a source does not make a fact so. Therefore quoting does not exempt you from libel.

These are just a few of the many reasons why you need to become familiar with all the aspects of libel, the rules laid down by the Federal Communication Commission, the Federal Trade Commission, and those special rules made by courts and agencies. Until you are sure about what is permitted, be as accurate as you can. And when in doubt, ask someone who knows. Knowing all the answers yourself is the surest way to get taken to court.

RADIO AND TELEVISION NEWS

There are no "absolute" rules governing the writing of news reports for oral presentation, whether for radio or for television. There are only customary, traditional, or convenient ways of doing it. The format and style differentiations will vary from station to station. Differences in news formats and the number of news items in a newcast also vary from station to station. They also vary from network to network. NBC presents news differently from CBS, CBS presents news differently from ABC, and ABC presents news differently from the Cable News Network. And by accident or design, news on a local station is presented differently from all the others. In general, these differences are governed by each outlet's news standards and by the ability and experience of each station's news team.

Some Differences in Radio and Television News

News reports heard on radio and television stations are alike in many respects. The basic differences between news stories that are written for radio and for television are mechanical, such as the amount of time given to a radio news report in comparison with a television news report. The time devoted to a story on radio is far less than that on television, because the majority of radio newscasts are five minutes long while most television newscasts, except for updates, are thirty minutes long. A few television newscasts are one hour long, and some are two hours. This means that the television newswriter can go into greater depth and detail than can a radio newswriter. Obviously the radio newswriter has to learn to say more in fewer words.

Another mechanical difference between radio and television news is that television listener-viewers can be taken by audiotape, film, or microwave from the news studio to the scene of the H-O-E-O. This same immediacy is supplied differently to radio listeners. For example, in addition to a radio news story the writer for that medium also tries to have available audiotape *actualities*. These are statements made by a person involved in the H-O-E-O.

Radio also tries to have a few *voicers*. A voicer is a reporter speaking via telephone from wherever the H-O-E-O is taking place. This may be a live report or it may be taped. The actuality and the voicer give the radio listener a feeling of being present at the scene of the H-O-E-O.

Writing and Time in a Newscast

Knowing how much to write for a radio newscast is a matter of simple arithmetic. The writer, or newscaster, begins with the total time available. If the total radio newscast is five minutes, the total time is 300 seconds. From those 300 seconds is subtracted the number of seconds needed for the opening and the closing remarks. Next the amount of time needed for the commercials is subtracted. The remaining time will be the number of seconds available for actualities, voicers, and news copy. After subtracting the time needed to run the voicers and the actualities, the writer then knows exactly how many seconds he has to fill with radio news copy.

Writing a television news story for a newscast also requires simple arithmetic. However, the specific details of a television news format are different and more complicated, because these details vary from station to station. Usually the newswriter is given the specific amount of time the story must fill. That may be his or her total contribution. When this occurs, timing involves story details rather than the total newscast. These story details will involve the inclusion of videotape and microexcerpts, a technique you should learn in production.

There are several reasons for not following a specific station format in a writing class. Most stations use a larger-size type on their copy typewriters. This large-size type helps the television newscaster to see the copy better and make fewer verbal errors. Some stations also use uppercase only when typing the newscaster's copy. Some stations use a larger upper- and lowercase.

Another specific difference between television formats is that some stations want the copy typed on the right half of the sheet and some want it typed in the middle of the sheet. Some television news formats require that the copy be typed in a certain size type in upper- and lowercase and have twenty-three character lines down the center of the $8\frac{1}{2}$-×-11-inch sheet of paper, with a total of eighteen triple-spaced lines per page. This means the twenty-three-letter-character-line page can be read in approximately twenty seconds, which times out with a comparable footage of videotape. The reason for this format is to help the news editor and the writer more easily judge the time relationship between the copy time and the video time.

If you currently need to perfect your writing skills—sentence structure, typing, spelling, punctuation, paragraphing—as well as all the other aspects involved in writing a news story, you will find it advantageous to follow a standard script format instead of a specialized station style. Certainly this will help you concentrate on writing.

That is why the following script format is recommended for your class assignments.

- Use a typewriter with pica type. Type your copy in upper- and lowercase. Upper- and lowercase forces one to be more literate. Research also indicates that upper- and lowercase is easier to read on a teleprompter. As a result, most stations are using enlarged upper- and lowercase instead of all caps as they once did. Therefore, you will be getting a head start in this direction.

- Use standard $8\frac{1}{2}$-×-11-inch typing paper. Most instructors prefer yellow paper. It is less expensive and does not reflect light in the eyes of the reader.

- Use a margin of $1\frac{1}{4}$ inches at the left side and at the bottom of the page. Use a 1-inch margin at the right side. This margin will vary some because you must never split a word.

- Place the complete identification requested by your instructor in the upper left corner of each sheet. This should be about 1 inch from the top of the page. This identification may consist of four or five single-spaced items of information, including your name.

- Begin typing your assignment an adequate distance below the identification.

- Always double space your copy and write on one side of the paper only.

- You can determine the time-length of your news story by multiplying the number of complete lines by four seconds per line. This is an approximation based on a reading speed of 150 to 155 words per minute. Note that this timing procedure is for your class work only.

- One story to a page.

ASSIGNMENTS

Listen to radio and television newscasts and list a representative sampling of news stories that have one or more of the six news factors.

List each factor that you hear in the order of its importance in the story. On a scale of 1 to 9, rank the importance of each factor found in each story.

List whether each news story you select is local, state, regional, national, or international.

Also note the specific differences in the way radio and television news is presented. One way to compare their differences is to close your eyes as you listen to TV news. This will help you decide whether the visual is essential to understanding the story.

CHAPTER 3

Developing a Newswriter's Style

POLICY AND PRACTICE

Each radio and television station has a news policy. This news policy guides that station's news team. It is usually handed to you in booklet form when you first join the staff. The purpose of the policy is to help assure the success of a station's news program.

Before you join a station be sure to learn all you can by listening to its news broadcasts. Note particularly the emphasis and slant of the morning, noon, and evening news. Each of these broadcasts will give you an indication of the station's news practices in relation to its coverage area.

However, the ability to write news must be taken with you to your first job. Furthermore, your writing techniques and ability should be fairly well established by that time. In other words, you should be ready and willing to fulfill your responsibility to the news organization that you join.

Here, then, to help you get ready for that first job are ways of conquering many difficult writing problems.

IMMEDIACY

There is one basic rule about writing news that everyone must follow. That rule is that every Happening, Occurrence, Event, or Occasion (H-O-E-O) must be told in such a way that it will hold the listener-viewer's attention. Writing that has a high interest value may be said to approximate the attitude that most normal human beings have toward their own existence. While every person has some interest in what happened yesterday, generally speaking, unless yesterday haunts the individual through the night, he or she remembers it as so much water under the dam. That is perhaps why few of us can give a moment-by-moment account of what was taking place where and why, twenty-four hours earlier.

Psychologically, all human beings are more interested in moment-by-moment activity because what is happening right now helps determine what each person may be doing next, including tomorrow. For example, most people respond physically and emotionally to the sound of a fire truck, a police or ambulance siren, a large explosion, and, until lately, a call for help. In other words, each person's instinctive reaction toward his own survival, and the survival of those he loves, causes him to be interested in the immediacy of each moment.

THE PRESENT TENSE

As a result of each person's instinctive desire to survive, every H-O-E-O is more interesting when it is told in the present tense. Present tense writing helps each listener-viewer live each H-O-E-O as if the outcome determines the future. That is why a news story written in the present tense will hold the listener-viewer's attention. It does this by linking the actor or the activity (the who and the what) of the H-O-E-O to the immediate moment. Most successful newswriters coordinate this relationship by stating the who, the what, and the when of the H-O-E-O in the very beginning of the story. This beginning statement in a news story is called the *lead*.

Combining the who and the what with the when in the lead is a relatively simple technique because the action of an H-O-E-O must always be related to the specific time when it occurs.

TENSE: DEFINITIONS AND USAGE

The writer's use of action as it relates to time is referred to in news reporting as *tense*. There are six definitions concerning the use of time that you as a beginning writer should first memorize and then review regularly until you can use each one intuitively.

Definition One When you write about a Happening, Occurrence, Event, or Occasion (H-O-E-O) taking place right now, you are writing about it in the present tense. For example:

1. Ladies and gentlemen. Here is the President of the United States.
2. The President is now speaking to a joint session of Congress.

Definition Two When you write about an H-O-E-O that has already taken place, you are writing about it in what is called the past tense. For example:

1. Ladies and gentlemen. The President of the United States was here yesterday.
2. Yesterday the President spoke to a joint session of Congress.

Definition Three When you write about an H-O-E-O that will take place some time in the future, you write about it in what is called the future tense. For example:

1. Ladies and gentlemen. The President of the United States will be here tomorrow morning.
2. Tomorrow morning the President will speak to a joint session of Congress.

Definition Four When you write about an H-O-E-O that has been completed by the present time, you write about it in what is called the present perfect tense. For example:

1. Ladies and gentlemen. The President of the United States has gone into the East Room.
2. The President has finished making his talk to the joint session of Congress and has gone to the White House.

Definition Five When you write about an H-O-E-O that was completed at some certain time in the past, you write about it in what is called the past perfect tense. For example:

1. Ladies and gentlemen. The President of the United States had gone into the East Room when the incident occurred.
2. The President had finished making his talk to the joint session of Congress and had gone back to the White House when you arrived.

Definition Six When you write about an H-O-E-O that will take place by some certain time in the future, you write about it in what is called the future perfect tense. For example:

1. Ladies and gentlemen. The President of the United States will have arrived by this time tomorrow.

2. The President will have finished making his speech to the joint session of Congress by the time the foreign dignitaries arrive.

After you check these six different ways of writing about an H-O-E-O, you will notice that news is more interesting when it is reported as it occurs. That's because, generally speaking, *news is now!* Therefore to capture the illusion that an H-O-E-O is taking place right now, professional writers use the present tense when writing for radio and television. Naturally, when something is happening as of this moment, writing in the present tense is the logical thing to do. And psychologically it is the most interesting way to tell a story to the listener-viewer.

The following opening of a news story illustrates the present tense technique:

> THE EGYPTIAN PRESIDENT, HOSNI MUBARAK, IS LANDING AT THE
> LEONARDO DA VINCI AIRPORT IN ROME.

This present tense statement emphasizes the immediacy of what is happening. At this time, at this very moment, while the listener-viewer is tuned in, the Egyptian President is landing at an airport in Rome.

Here is a second story in the present tense. Note how easy it is to write the story in the past tense, a common practice by many beginning writers. All you do to create past tense is to write the verb *was* instead of *is*.

> A FIRE **IS** RAGING IN THE HILLS OVERLOOKING LOS ANGELES. IT **IS** OUT
> OF CONTROL BECAUSE A FIFTY-MILE-AN-HOUR WIND **IS** CAUSING
> HOMES TO IGNITE LIKE KINDLING WOOD.

Even though news is at its best when it is reported as it happens, in the present tense, all news events do not occur that conveniently for the radio-television newswriter. When a newswriter faces the fact that an event has not occurred for his convenience, he must shift to the tense that is appropriate. As an example of this problem, let us finish the story about Egyptian President Hosni Mubarak's flight to Rome.

When we consider the rest of the events relating to Mubarak's landing at the airport, we see that other things will be happening in the near future. What is Mubarak going to do in Rome? That is future tense.

> THE EGYPTIAN PRESIDENT, HOSNI MUBARAK, IS LANDING AT THE
> LEONARDO DA VINCI AIRPORT IN ROME. A MOTORCADE IS STANDING
> BY TO RUSH THE EGYPTIAN PRESIDENT TO THE VATICAN WHERE HE

WILL CONFER WITH POPE JOHN PAUL FOR AN HOUR BEFORE FLYING
ON TO LONDON TO ADDRESS THE BRITISH PARLIAMENT.

Now, as the story is written, it begins in the present, present tense,
and then switches to what is to come, future tense. This shift is necessary
to let the listener-viewer know why Mubarak is landing in Rome. What
Mubarak will do after he visits the Pope is a future event still unknown to
the listener-viewer. To furnish some of this information the writer digs into
the past and continues his story as follows:

JUST BEFORE THE EGYPTIAN LEADER TOOK OFF FROM CAIRO,
REPORTERS LEARNED THAT PRESIDENT MUBARAK HAS BEEN
PLANNING THIS TRIP FOR TWO YEARS.

Note how the writer uses tense in this part of the story. By and large,
the closer the writer can keep his story to the present tense, the more
interesting it will be to hear. However, do not overdo the use of present
tense just to liven up your story. If you do, it may become ridiculous. In
other words, never force a story into an unnatural combination of tenses.
    What this all means is that while you avoid using the past tense as
much as possible, the fact is that some stories are best told in the past
tense. For example, here is part of a story told in the present tense that
should definitely be told in the past tense.

A PEDESTRIAN IS KILLED BY A HIT-AND-RUN DRIVER IN OLD
SAVANNAH LAST NIGHT.

The conflict between the present tense statement "is killed" and the
past tense statement "last night" calls attention to the conflict between the
action and the time. This conflict causes the listener-viewer's attention to
be directed toward how the message is said rather than toward what is
said. That is why professional writers of such a story would select the past
tense, "was killed." Its use is more logical than forcing the story's events
into an awkward time sequence that is contrary to fact.
    Some news reports, as illustrated by the Mubarak story, may profit
from a mixture of present, past, and future tenses. Mixing tenses is permitted under these circumstances as long as the mixing does not call attention
to itself.
    Always keep in mind that news reporting is considered to be a process
that is happening as of the moment. It is taking place right now. That is
the basic reason news should be written in the present tense. This tense
helps the listener-viewer visualize what is happening. Writing in the
present tense also helps cut down on the time it takes the writer to tell a
story. Saving time on the air is one of the most important contributions

a writer can make to broadcasting because both radio and television exist by selling program time.

Your ability to communicate as a writer is the investment you make in program time. The return on that investment is the number of listener-viewers tuned in.

"VOICE" IN NEWS

Another way a writer can increase listener-viewer interest in a news story is to write it in the *active voice*. Active voice involves verb usage in each sentence. Here are three definitions that will help you understand this important aspect of writing.

First: A verb is any word or group of words that express action, existence, occurrence, or state of being.

Second: A verb is in the active voice when the subject of a sentence (that which, or whom, you are writing about) *does the acting*. For example:

1. The rightfielder is catching the flyball.
2. The crowd is laughing at the senator's joke.
3. The beauty queen is singing the national anthem.
4. The first batter strikes out.

Note the order of the words in each of these active voice statements. The subject, the person doing the acting in each statement, is:

1. rightfielder
2. crowd
3. beauty queen
4. batter

The verb in each of these sentences, indicating how each subject acted, is:

1. catching
2. laughing
3. singing
4. strikes out

Because each statement is in the active voice, the meaning is specific and direct. It creates a feeling that an action is being performed.

Third: A verb is in the *passive voice* when the subject (that which, or whom, you are writing about) is *acted upon*. For example:

1. The ball is caught by the rightfielder.
2. The senator's joke is laughed at by the crowd.

3. The national anthem is sung by the beauty queen.
4. The first batter is struck out.

Note how the order of the words in each passive voice sentence slows down the thought process and also the visualization. It does this because the subject in each sentence is being acted upon instead of doing the acting. When the action is slowed down this way, the listener-viewer needs more time in which to understand what is happening.

A statement in the passive voice also implies that the action has already taken place instead of occurring at the moment, as it does when the active voice is used.

In summary, all top writers use the active voice to communicate a closer proximity to the action. Active voice is also more specific.

SPECIFICITY AND NEWS

When you select a verb to describe a specific action, you should avoid selecting one that is overworked. For example, does the batter always "strike out"? Does he always knock in a "home run"? When two cars make contact at an intersection, how do you describe that meeting? The words "accident" and "crash," both overworked, are used to describe most cars that meet in such a manner.

There are many verbs that can be substituted for your favorite ones. For example, when you see someone wearing shorts and shoes whose body is falling forward but is kept erect by first one leg and then the other swinging forward, how do you describe what he is doing? Is he dashing, fleeing, jogging, streaking, moving, plodding, pursuing, running, sprinting, traveling, trotting, walking, or what?

It is extremely important that a writer use the exact word to indicate the specific action taking place. How do you describe what someone said? Many writers use the word "said." Grammatically the word "said" is the past tense of "say." But neither word is specific. Each is a neutral word and means to "express in words."

Selecting a specific word is of major importance. Many times, however, your substitute will give you an entirely different meaning. To illustrate this problem let us take a simple statement with the word "says" in it instead of the past tense "said":

TWO SENATORS SAY THE COUNTRY IS HEADED FOR A DEPRESSION.

To determine whether "say" is the best word to use, we next collect other words that are considered to be synonymous with it. Here is a list of synonyms and a partial definition for each:

1. acknowledge—to admit what we are saying or doing.
2. add—we make an additional statement as an afterthought.
3. admit—we acknowledge a point made against us or someone else.
4. allege—to declare, to affirm, to assert positively without proof.
5. announce—to formally make a public statement about something.
6. answer—to reply or to respond to a question.
7. assert—to make a strongly personal statement, usually positive. It may imply a lack of proof or accuracy.
8. aver—to declare positively that which we are certain of from our own knowledge.
9. claim—we request our baggage and our rights.
10. concede—we yield to a rightful request or compelling claim.
11. confess—we admit to our faults or the errors of our ways.
12. contend—to hold, to assert something is a fact.
13. declare—an authoritative and formal statement.
14. deny—to declare that something reportedly said is untrue.
15. disclose—to reveal something that is not generally known.
16. divulge—a public disclosure with the suggestion of a breach of confidence.
17. emphasize—to forcefully stress a point in order to call attention to it.
18. grant—a voluntary acknowledgment.
19. maintain—a firm, persistent upholding of something as being true, when it may not be true.
20. proclaim—an authoritative and formal public declaration.
21. profess—to make a public declaration or acknowledgment.
22. promise—a pledge that an agreement will be met.
23. reiterate—to repeat or say something again.
24. refute—to disprove.
25. remark—to make a brief statement taking notice of or referring to an observation.
26. repeat—to reiterate that which was said before.
27. report—to make an account of or state an opinion of a decision.
28. state—to declare, propound, or specify in a formal or definite manner.
29. stress—to emphasize something we say by making a special point or utterance.
30. vow—to declare or solemnly affirm or assert a promise.

The next step in making a word choice is to discover how many of the synonyms selected can be used to replace the original word. The question here is how many of these thirty-two synonyms can be used to replace "say" and make the sentence more meaningful, more specific.

We determine this by studying the definitions and discovering that some of these synonyms are not appropriate. Obviously some of them communicate a condition that is contrary to fact. Therefore to discover the specific use of each we classify them into three groups: Group 1—those synonyms we know we cannot use; Group 2—those synonyms we might be able to use; Group 3—those synonyms that seem appropriate to replace the word "say" in the original sentence, Two senators say the country is headed for a depression.

Group 1	*Group 2*	*Group 3*
acknowledge	assert	declare
add	contend	state
admit	emphasize	warn
allege	maintain	
announce	reiterate	
answer	remark	
aver	stress	
claim		
confess		
deny		
disclose		
divulge		
grant		
proclaim		
profess		
promise		
refute		
repeat		
report		
reveal		
utter		
vow		

One of the problems with regard to finding a synonym for "say" is that it is a neutral verb. Its use implies nothing about the senators or the message other than that they made the statement. Therefore what we have to ask ourselves as writers is: Are there ideas and concepts about the senators that should be communicated by using a different synonym for "say"? If we find one, will it change the what or the how of the statement? Will we be replacing the basic concept of what the senators meant to communicate?

When we consider the list of synonyms in Group 1, we see immediately that they will not do. Try some of them for laughs. The Group 2 list is better, but the ones in that list seem to comment on the way in which the senators made their remark. Even the Group 3 list may connote and denote meanings to the listener-viewer that are not appropriate for this occasion. It is true that on a different occasion one might write:

1. TWO SENATORS DECLARE THE COUNTRY IS HEADED FOR A DEPRESSION.

2. TWO SENATORS STATE THE COUNTRY IS HEADED FOR A DEPRESSION.

3. TWO SENATORS WARN THAT THE COUNTRY IS HEADED FOR A DEPRESSION.

There might even be a different occasion when one might write that the senators assert, contend, emphasize, maintain, reiterate, remark, or even stress that the country is headed for a depression. But it is not likely that they would ever confess, divulge, promise, or vow that such is the country's future.

The problem with finding a specific word for a specific meaning may seem very difficult. There may be other words than those in these lists that would do a more specific job. Be that as it may, the writer should always seek the word that will do the best job of communicating a specific meaning for a specific occasion, whatever it may be.

However, when you are searching for the specific word, don't overlook the fact that sometimes a newswriter must ignore all the lively and likely synonyms and settle for one that is strictly neutral. Here are two additional neutral synonyms that might be used for "say":

TWO SENATORS REPORT THE COUNTRY IS HEADED FOR A DEPRESSION.

TWO SENATORS TELL REPORTERS THE COUNTRY IS HEADED FOR A DEPRESSION.

Each of these words is neutral and will not distort the senators' meaning.

In summary, many times a neutral word choice can be improved. Many times it cannot. And on occasion the writer must select a neutral word to avoid the possibility of libel. But the writer who cares about his or her work will always consider how well a word "fits" the meaning with a view to using the one that does the best job of communicating a message to the listener-viewer. Remember, creating positive feedback is your goal. And that goal does not make the job of becoming a precise writer an easy one. But it is the way to become a professional writer.

NAMES AND TITLES

Names can be all important in a news story. You will recall that many times the name itself is the news. That is why the broadcast writer must learn to handle names carefully and efficiently.

When a name is unknown, or relatively so, the writer must set the scene before introducing the person by name. When the writer uses this technique the listener-viewer will feel more knowledgeable and identify more fully with the person involved in the H-O-E-O. For example:

A PHILADELPHIA PEDESTRIAN SAVED A DRIVER FROM CERTAIN DEATH
THIS NOON. THE PEDESTRIAN, CARL DOBBINS, WAS CROSSING SEVENTH
AND SIXTY-FOURTH ON HIS WAY TO LUNCH WHEN TWO CARS CRASHED
HEAD ON. ONE OF THE CARS BURST INTO FLAMES. AS ITS
UNCONSCIOUS DRIVER SLUMPED OVER THE WHEEL . . .

The writer of this story made it perfectly clear why the pedestrian is important in this story before his name was mentioned.

A well-known name is always good news. Nonetheless, it should be identified so that it is easily and instantly recognized by the listener-viewer.

It is also essential that identification be made clear because of the duplication of names and the fact that the name of a person prominent in one region may not be known in another region. And yet the nature of the news may be important to a second region or even to a third. Therefore the writer must be sure to use adequate identification.

However, when the news is important only in a specific area the writer's responsibility is easily taken care of, as follows:

JACKSONVILLE'S MAYOR JOHN BRENT JOINED THE FORCES
ADVOCATING A CONTINUATION OF THE INTRASTATE CANAL SYSTEM.
AT A MORNING NEWS CONFERENCE BRENT SAID THAT MORE THAN
THREE FLORIDA COUNTIES WOULD BENEFIT FROM THE SYSTEM'S
COMPLETION.

Written this way, the story is of importance to the coverage area only.

Many times the person's job, or his actions, are more meaningful to the listener-viewer than his name. For example:

FORMER PRESIDENT JIMMY CARTER . . .

CONGRESSMAN JOHN JONES . . .

PRESIDENT RONALD REAGAN . . .

Whether an individual's title is repeated after the first reference will depend upon the nature and structure of the story. Many stations are now dropping the requirement of calling the person Mr. after the initial identification. Check that requirement in your station's script guide and style manual. For example:

PRESIDENT REAGAN LEFT FOR ENGLAND THIS MORNING. REAGAN
HOPES TO MEET WITH LEADERS FROM ALL THE WESTERN EUROPEAN
NATIONS.

Sometimes the title that identifies the person is repeated:

PRESIDENT REAGAN HELD A CLOSED MEETING WITH THE WESTERN
EUROPEAN HEADS OF STATE ON THE OIL CRISIS TODAY. AFTER THE
MEETING, PRESIDENT REAGAN TOLD NEWSMEN THAT . . .

Mr., Mrs., and Ms.

When you are writing about a husband and wife it is customary to use Mr. and Mrs. After the first reference, the man's last name may be used instead. For example:

AN INDIANAPOLIS COUPLE WAS KILLED IN A TRUCK ACCIDENT SOUTH
OF CHICAGO TODAY. MR. AND MRS. THEODORE HUSING OF TWENTY-
TWO JACKSON DRIVE WERE IDENTIFIED AS THE VICTIMS. MRS. HUSING
WAS KILLED INSTANTLY. HUSING WAS PRONOUNCED DEAD ON
ARRIVAL AT A LOCAL COUNTY HOSPITAL.

Most females, after the initial identification, are referred to as Miss or Mrs. In many stations the identification Ms. is used when the person's name does not indicate whether she is Miss or Mrs. In some stations Ms. is never used unless it is requested by the woman involved. Some stations refuse to use Ms. because they contend that to do so is to treat women differently from men and that, they argue, is not equal rights for everyone. The use of a person's last name also varies from station to station. Therefore, become familiar with your station's script guide before you begin writing.

Identifying the Clergy

There are specific routines to be followed in identifying the clergy of different religious faiths. These routines are practiced both in the initial and the succeeding reference.

THE REVEREND DOUGLAS MATHEW (first reference)
REVEREND MATHEW (subsequent reference)

JEW
RABBI HARRY STEINMETZ (first reference)
RABBI STEINMETZ (subsequent reference)

ROMAN CATHOLIC
THE REVEREND THOMAS HIDDING (first reference)
FATHER HIDDING (subsequent reference)

SOURCE AND ATTRIBUTION

Detailed information about a Happening, Occurrence, Event, or Occasion (H-O-E-O) must come from somewhere. That somewhere is called a *source*.

A source is defined as that which is responsible for imparting information. A source is usually a person, but it may be a place or a thing.

The term *attribution* is also used in reference to sources by newswriters, and it means assigning, identifying, indicating, or crediting the information that is being used by the writer to a specific origin. For example:

PRESIDENT REAGAN WARNED CONGRESS THAT A LARGE BUDGET . . .

Identifying the person is a typical example of an attribution.

The writer's responsibility for being accurate when attributing can be a problem. The problem occurs most often when the writer is hurrying to meet a deadline. And because there is an urgent need for haste, he or she may not take the necessary time to check and recheck such simple details as the spelling of the source's name, the source's age, address, position, and responsibilities.

Always the writer must know the exact time when an H-O-E-O occurs. The writer must also know that the facts and figures involved are accurate. He or she must also be certain whether or not the information should be used in the story. The primary reason for having such information is that if it is not used in the original story there is the possibility that it may be needed in a follow-up story.

This need for accurate details is essential because listener-viewers will not trust newswriters who are inaccurate. Accuracy is equated with honesty. The lack of accuracy implies that the station is an unreliable news source. Furthermore, the lack of accuracy may cost the writer his or her job, just as inaccurate reporting may cause the station to become involved in a costly lawsuit. Therefore, one of the best ways to avoid misunderstanding is to have attribution precede the statement. For example:

ACCORDING TO MAYOR GLORIA BROWN,THE CITY OF CENTERVILLE IS
IN DIRE NEED OF PAVED STREETS.

Sometimes, however, a writer trying to achieve variety will unconsciously bury the attribution. Doing so may be misleading. As a result the writer may be accused of editorializing because the attribution is not perfectly clear. This confusion as to who said what occurs because the listener-viewer stops focusing attention on what is being said as soon as the statement is made. The following is an example of burying the attribution and increasing the possibility of being misunderstood:

THE CITY OF CENTERVILLE IS IN DIRE NEED OF ADDITIONAL PAVED
STREETS, SAYS MAYOR GLORIA BROWN.

Neither should the writer place the attribution in the middle of the statement. Doing so makes the story sound awkward because the attribution disrupts the listener-viewer's concentration. For example:

THE CITY OF CENTREVILLE, SAYS ITS MAYOR, IS IN DIRE NEED OF
ADDITIONAL PAVED STREETS.

In both radio and television news it is best to let the listener-viewers know who is talking before you tell them what is being said. This means the writer begins with an attribution.

But even this routine creates a problem, and that problem is monotony. Therefore, to avoid sounding monotonous and repetitious, many newswriters for radio and television use as little attribution as possible. And although the source of a statement who said it, is always important, it is true that attribution may be left out when it is not absolutely necessary for clarity.

On occasion monotony may be avoided by using more than one attribution phrase in a story. This is a relatively useful method because additional attribution in the same story not only adds variety, it tells the listener-viewer more about the source. For example:

FORMER SECRETARY OF STATE HENRY KISSINGER TOLD THE NATION
ON "MEET THE PRESS" TODAY THAT THIS COUNTRY NEEDS A BETTER
WAY OF COMMUNICATING FOREIGN POLICY THAN THROUGH THE
PRESS. THE FORMER HARVARD PROFESSOR SAID THE RECENT
BREAKDOWN IN COMMUNICATIONS WITH IRAN INDICATES THE NEED
TO DO MORE PRIVATE TALKING AND LESS PUBLIC TALKING.

Personal pronouns are a form of attribution. A broadcast newswriter must be careful when using them as a secondary attribution. When the pronoun reference is not perfectly clear, the listener-viewer may be unable to keep in mind who she, he, or they may be. This problem with the personal pronoun as an attribution is more difficult when there are two persons in a story. In this case, the writer must always be on the safe side of clarity and not hesitate to repeat the source's name, the primary attribution. Clarity is basic to quality broadcast writing, regardless of repetitiousness or monotony. For example:

SECRETARY OF STATE GEORGE SCHULTZ BEGAN HIS SHUTTLE
DIPLOMACY WEDNESDAY BY MEETING WITH ISRAEL'S PRIME MINISTER
MENACHEM BEGIN. SCHULTZ ON HIS ARRIVAL FROM CAIRO WENT
IMMEDIATELY TO . . .

THE USE OF ABBREVIATIONS

The use of initials to represent well-known organizations has become a part of our language and a part of our lives. As a result, the full title for the name of a familiar organization need not always be used when referring to it even the first time. Each broadcast station has its own regulations for its writers to follow. In general, however, you will find that rule number one is always to use full identification if there is the slightest doubt about whether the initials are familiar to the listener-viewers.

When abbreviations are used to replace long and involved titles, be sure to separate each letter from the others with a hyphen. This is specifically necessary if it is to be read one letter at a time. For example:

U-N, H-E-W, F-B-I, U-A-W, G-O-P, Y-M-C-A, A-F-L, Y-W-C-A, U-S, I-O-U, F-S-C,
U-S-S-R, C-I-A, N-A-A-C-P

(Avoid writing N-double-A-C-P because that takes longer to say even though it is easier.)

The initials for many organizations and institutions are so well known they have become words. These are called acronyms. Each is written so it can and will be pronounced as a word. For example:

NATO, NASA PATCO, TOPS, HUD, SEATO, AID, CORE, OPEC

The general rule in many stations about abbreviations is "Don't use them." However, some titles for people are abbreviated when written, but are given full pronunciation when they are spoken by the newscaster. For example:

DR., MR., MRS., ST. LOUIS, ST. PAUL

QUOTATIONS

The presence of a quotation in a radio or television news story tends to disrupt the thought flow in the report. That is why a writer should, in-so-far as is possible, paraphrase what ordinarily would be quoted. Paraphrasing also makes the story more specific and concise. As you know, specificity is of vital importance in all news communication.

Furthermore, the use of the terms "quote" and "unquote" in a news story is cumbersome and lacking in finesse. Therefore, when a quote is necessary, the newswriter helps the newscaster by making the quote as short as possible. Lengthy quotes, like lengthy sentences, handicap most newscasters as well as most listener-viewers.

One way of solving the quote problem is to organize your copy so that the newscaster can indicate a quote is to be given. This he can do with a pause or by making a specific shift in his vocal pitch or intensity. The writer indicates these pauses and shifts by using the three dot ellipsis (. . .) in the copy. Even direct quotes can be communicated by such pauses.

Paraphrases are managed by preparing the listener-viewers with a special phrase. For example:

THE GENERAL WENT ON TO SAY . . .

THE MAYOR ADDED THIS WARNING . . .

IN HIS WORDS . . .

AS THE PRESIDENT TOLD REPORTERS . . .

CONTRACTIONS

In regular conversation our language falls into a melody created by the stressing and the unstressing of words. This stress pattern is based on the fact that all words carrying special meanings are stressed according to their importance in relation to what we are saying. Words that carry secondary meanings and words that merely help hold ideas together are unstressed by being rushed over lightly, or barely sounded. As a result of this tendency to stress and unstress in the communication of meaning, some words get pulled together, *contracted*, and in the process literally form a new word.

Writing news for the purpose of communicating it orally requires the use of a number of these contracted words to help the newscaster do a better job of telling the listener-viewer about an H-O-E-O. The use of contractions also helps the newscaster sound less stilted and less formal. Therefore it is the responsibility of the newswriter to prepare copy that helps the newscaster sound his best. Here are a few contraction examples in general use:

do not—don't	he would—he'd
does not—doesn't	is not—isn't
has not—hasn't	they are—they're
he is—he's	will not—won't
he will—he'll	would not—wouldn't

However, certain word contractions are not useful over the air because they disrupt the newscaster's flow of language and cause his speech to sound choppy and awkward. For example, "It will" is one. Do not write "It'll."

The writer should also avoid contractions whose use weakens the story or whose presence in the copy calls attention to the writing.

Many reputable broadcast newswriters, and stations, never use contractions because they believe a story that is important enough to be on the air should be written in language that is semiformal and is therefore worthy of the job it has been selected to do. It is well for the beginner to avoid contractions until told to do otherwise.

NUMBERS AND STATISTICS

Symbols for numbers, statistics, and money have become so much a part of our daily lives that a systematic way of communicating them is essential in all electronic communication. As a writer, you may find yourself writing about weekend and holiday death statistics. You may also spend hours sifting through sports statistics, as well as money market and stock market reports.

The general rule about numbers, statistics, and money figures is that the more of these used, the more complex and less communicable your report becomes. As a result, use as few numbers and statistics as possible. Remember, a three- or four-digit number causes most newscasters to stumble. These complicated numbers also confuse the listener-viewer.

The following procedure is customarily used by top radio and television writers:

1. Write out numbers one through nine.

2. Because the number eleven may cause a problem, many spell it out. Some stations have their writers spell out all numbers from one through eleven.

3. It is general practice to use figures for numbers 10 through 999. This usage also applies to dates, time, and sports scores. After 999, spell out the basic units.

4. When the factual content of a story is not seriously affected, it is customary to round off all figures of 100 or more. For example: 862,092 becomes 862 thousand, or more than 860 thousand; 1,096 becomes almost

11 hundred; 1,200 becomes 12 hundred; 13,000 becomes 13 thousand; 14,000,000 becomes 14 million; 15,500 becomes 15-thousand-500.

The reason for writing large numbers in words instead of figures is to help the listener-viewer concentrate on the story rather than on translating the zeroes into hundreds, thousands, millions, or even billions.

5. When a sentence is begun with a number (not a desirable practice in newswriting), the number *must* be spelled out. For example: *Four hundred thousand cheering fans crowded the stadium.*

6. Always avoid the use of "A" for "one" when writing a large number. Instead, write *one hundred, one thousand, one million.* On the air "A" too often sounds like "eight."

7. Four digits are used to indicate the year: *1985,* not *'85; 1776,* not *'76.*

8. Fractions and decimals are always spelled out: *two and one-half,* not $2\frac{1}{2}$. Write *six-tenths,* not *0.06; fourteen-point-seven billion,* not *14.7 billion.* In general, decimals are not used in broadcast copy.

9. Numerals are used for ages. When writing ages, do not follow the newspaper style of writing. Instead, put the numerals before the name and combine them with a hyphen. For example: *The Governor's 18-year-old son was admitted to the hospital July 8th. He was . . .*

10. The number of each day of the month should be followed with its appropriate *st, nd, rd,* or *th.* Also the month and its day should be written in a way that makes it easier for the newscaster to verbalize that information in a message. For example, it is much easier to say *September 4th* or the *fourth of Septemper* than it is to say *September 4* or *four September.*

11. Always write addresses with numerals. For example: *1708 Myrick Road* or *124 Main Street.* However, when the street's name is a numeral— *8th Street, 10th Street,* etc.—spell out the number. Example: *1258 Tenth Street.*

12. On occasion the division of the day into A.M. and P.M. becomes important to a story. When this occurs, A.M. or P.M. is indicated by writing *in the morning, before noon, in the evening,* or whatever it may be.

13. Do not force the newscaster to mentally translate what a specific symbol means. Always translate it for him into a spelled-out word. For example, instead of using @, write *each;* instead of #, write *number;* for $, write *dollar;* for %, write *percent;* for ¢, write *cent;* for +, write *plus;* for =, write *equals.* Examples: 14 *dollars and ten cents; 15 percent; each oil tanker costs more than four and one half million dollars.*

14. A statistic or a percentage may be confusing to the newscaster, and the listener-viewer, as to exactly how much it really is. When this may be the case, the writer must explain what is meant in the news report. For example:

THE WISCONSIN LEGISLATURE IS PROPOSING AN ADDITIONAL ONE-MILL
TAX ON ALL PROPERTY IN THE STATE. A ONE-MILL TAX LEVY WILL
ADD FIVE DOLLARS TO THE YEARLY PROPERTY TAX ON A
40-THOUSAND-DOLLAR HOME, AND BRING IN AN ADDITIONAL 50-
MILLION DOLLARS TO THE STATE'S GENERAL REVENUE FUND.

15. Finally, when the writer is having a problem making a statistic or a number meaningful and relevant to the listener-viewer, he or she should consult his or her superior.

PUNCTUATION

Punctuation is a form of sign language that is used to help make clear what you write. It is a way of adding meaning. We use two kinds of punctuation. One set of punctuation marks is used for copy that is to be read silently, and another set of punctuation marks is used for writing copy that is to be spoken aloud. Because writing for broadcasting is to be read aloud, a punctuation system especially for use with it has been developed. For example, a broadcast writer avoids using:

1. the colon
2. the semicolon
3. the exclamation mark
4. the question mark

Using them tends to confuse the newscaster when he reads a story aloud.

The most useful punctuation marks for radio and television newswriting and newscasting are:

1. the comma
2. the period
3. the hyphen or dash
4. the ellipsis (three periods in a row: ...)

The ellipsis sign, the dash, and the hyphen are each used in broadcast newswriting for specific purposes. The three-dot ellipsis may be used instead of a comma for the following reasons:

1. The ellipsis indicates to the newscaster when a breath pause may be taken without interrupting or interfering with the thought processes in a story. Use of the ellipsis is recommended when the newscaster is to read the copy cold and needs all the help he can get from the writer. For example:

THE CONGRESSMAN . . . IN HIS TALK BEFORE THE JOINT SESSION OF
THE INDIANA LEGISLATURE . . . WARNED IT AGAINST EXCESSIVE
APPROPRIATIONS. HE SAID . . . LEGISLATURES IN EVERY STATE MUST
BEAR SOME OF THE BURDEN FOR INFLATION.

2. To indicate where the announcer may make a phrase stand out by changing his pitch or vocal emphasis through the use of inflection. For example:

THE HOUSTON OILERS 24, THE RAMS 9 . . . THE MIAMI DOLPHINS 14, NEW
YORK JETS 2.

3. To indicate that the opening phrase of a sentence is a prepositional phrase and should be given special vocal consideration. For example:

IN NORTHERN MAINE . . .

MEANWHILE . . . IN CALIFORNIA . . . THE CAMPAIGN FOR UNSEATING
THE GOVERNOR RECEIVED A NEW SETBACK . . .

4. The hyphen and its use have already been introduced under abbreviations. It is used to indicate to the announcer that certain letter groupings and certain number groupings are to be read one at a time. For example:

ONE C-I-A SPOKESMAN SAYS . . .
BEVERLY WILDE . . . THAT'S SPELLED W-I-L-D-E . . .

The hyphen is used in regular writing at the end of a page line to indicate that a word has been divided or split. In broadcast newswriting a word is never split at the end of a line. However, some word combinations are easier for the announcer to read aloud if they are hyphenated. Many stations want their newswriters to hyphenate words that begin with such prefixes as *anti, co, non*, and *semi*, even though the words are not spelled that way. The use of the hyphen helps the newscaster. For example:

ANTI-ESTABLISHMENT	ANTI-SOCIAL
CO-EDUCATION	CO-DEFENDANT
NON-INJURIOUS	NON-MEMBER
SEMI-CONDUCTOR	SEMI-DETACHED

Numbers spelled out are also hyphenated to signal the newscaster not to pause. For example:

THE FIVE-YEAR-OLD
TEN-TO-ONE CHANCE
EIGHT-POINT-TWO
THE ODDS ARE NINE-TO-FIVE

This kind of visual aid is of special help to announcers and news-casters. However, always avoid letting such a hyphen come at the end of a line of copy. Doing so may defeat your purpose.

PRONUNCIATION GUIDE

The most systematic way to determine how a word may be written so that it will be pronounced accurately is to employ *phonetic symbols*. Phonetics is a system of written symbols for speech sounds. These sounds are heard in all languages. In fact, the system is so valuable to the study of language in all countries that an international phonetic alphabet has been developed. However, the use of this alphabet by broadcasters is impractical because of the amount of time it takes to understand the system and learn to use it.

There is, however, another phonetic system based on phonics. This system can be, and is, used by broadcast writers. Phonics is also the name given to the method used in teaching most beginning grade-school children to read and pronounce words in terms of the sound value assigned to the vowels and the consonants in our language. Because everyone is already familiar with the so-called five vowels and eight consonants used in this phonic system, its general use has been widely adopted by news services, even though an occasional word does not lend itself to an accurate pronunciation via this system. Regardless of such problems, the system can be mastered so quickly that every broadcast wire service uses it. The following is all the broadcast writer needs to have as a reference for it.*

Vowels

A. Use AY for long A as in m*a*te.
    A for short A as in c*a*t.
    AI for nasal A as in *ai*r.
    AH for short A as in f*a*ther.
    AW for broad A as in t*a*lk.
E. Use EE for long E as in m*ee*t.
    EH for short E as in b*e*t.
    UH for hollow E as in th*e* or l*e* (French article).

* See United Press International, *Stylebook* (New York: 1981).

AY for French E with accent as in pathé.

IH for E as in pretty.

EW for E as in few.

I. Use EYE for long I as in time.

EE for French long I as in machine.

IH for short I as in pity.

O. Use OH for long O as in note, or *ough* as in th*ough*.

AH for short O as in hot.

AW for broad O as in fought.

OO for O as in fool, or *ough* as in thr*ough*.

U for O as in foot.

UH for *ouch* as in touch.

OW for O as in how, or *ough* as in pl*ough*.

U. Use EW for long U as in mule.

OO for long U as in rule.

U for middle U as in put.

UH for short U as in shut.

Consonants

Use K for hard C as in cat.

S for soft C as in cease.

SH for soft CH as in machine.

CH for hard CH or TCH as in catch.

Z for hard S as in disease.

S for soft S as in sun.

G for hard G as in gang.

J for soft G as in general.

The Phonetic Pronouncer

It is always the responsibility of the writer to insert the correct pronunciation in copy immediately following the word in question. Be sure to place the pronunciation in parentheses and divide the word into syllables. The syllable or syllables that should be accented are typed in caps. For example:

TWO AMERICAN TOURISTS FROM LIMA (LIGH-mah), OHIO, WERE
ACCIDENTLY KILLED IN LIMA (LEE-mah), PERU, LAST NIGHT.

DURING A TWO-DAY BLIZZARD, SNOW REACHED A DEPTH OF 24-
INCHES IN YAKIMA (YAK-uh-maw) AND WALLA WALLA, WASHINGTON.

SIXTY MEMBERS OF THE CHAMBER OF COMMERCE FROM CAIRO (KAY-
roh), ILLINOIS, FLEW TO CAIRO (KEYE-roh), EGYPT, TODAY.

Pronouncers, as they are called in broadcast news, help the newscaster read his copy smoothly and without abrupt pauses. Hesitations while the newscaster determines the correct pronunciation can cause the credibility of a station's reporters to be questioned. Correct pronunciation is such an important aspect of news that wire services provide a list of pronouncers each day and give in detail the names of foreign places and new people appearing in the news. Wire services also include national and regional names and places if the particular pronunciation is not well known.

One final suggestion about each pronouncer you put in your copy. Be sure to call the pronunciation to the attention of the newscaster before he goes on the air. You should do this because you are the final authority responsible for seeing that the pronunciation is handled smoothly and correctly.

CHAPTER **4**

Writing
Broadcast
News

GETTING STARTED

There are many ways to develop a news story from information about a Happening, an Occurrence, an Event, or an Occasion. While you will later use a fact-finding procedure for the specific purpose of collecting information, at present what you need can be found by using the 5 Ws and H formula. The majority of professional writers have been using this formula for a long time. As Rudyard Kipling (1865–1936) wrote in his "The Elephant Child,"

> *I keep six honest serving men,*
> *(they taught me all I knew);*
> *Their names are* what *and* why *and* when
> *And* how *and* where *and* who.

For your purpose let's rearrange them to read *who*, *what*, *when*, *where*, *why*, and *how*.

Because time limitations keep most broadcast messages short, you will rarely use all the information provided by asking and finding answers to

40

more than two or three of these six questions: who, what, when, where, why, and how. That is why after considering the most important questions in terms of the facts available about an H-O-E-O, you will have enough information to develop a news story.

UNDERSTANDING THE LEAD

Each broadcast news story must be written in such a way that the listener-viewer's attention is caught and held. This makes news reporting an intensely personal matter even though the writer must remain objective. Objectivity in newswriting is an acquired ability. It is the result of under-standing and using various writing techniques. The first of these is sentence structure.

All forms of newswriting teach that grammatically a sentence is a group of related words that convey a complete thought. Such a sentence has in it, either expressed or implied, a subject and a predicate. In addition, sentence structures may be simple, complex, or compound. However, the broadcast news sentence is more successful when it is simple. This is particularly true of the news *lead*, the first sentence in your news story.

The term lead is newswriting jargon. It is used in all newsroom areas and wire service quarters. The lead as a device was developed years ago as a special way of starting a news story. Its purpose is to state a specific aspect of the total information that is available. This is a brief initial statement of what your story is all about. In other words, your lead will embody or imply a thesis, theme, or central idea that is related to a problem, need, feeling, or desire. That is why your story must be developed and constructed around this lead.

Sometimes in a broadcast news story the lead is more than one sentence. But whatever the length, the broadcast news lead must state a specific aspect of the total information available. Therefore, it must be a statement and not a headline. For example:

HEADLINE:
LOCAL BANK ROBBED.

LEAD:
THREE MASKED GUNMEN HELD UP THE DOWNTOWN BRANCH OF THE
CITIZENS FIRST NATIONAL BANK AT NOON TODAY.
or
AT NOON TODAY THREE MEN WEARING MASKS ROBBED THE CITIZENS
FIRST NATIONAL BANK.

Regardless of the order of events included in the lead, the specific words the writer chooses are determined by the nature of the Happening, Occurrence, Event, or Occasion. It is in this way that the lead can reflect the H-O-E-O's relationship to the listener-viewer. This relationship is important because plain facts said dully will not keep the listener-viewer tuned to that particular station. Listener-viewers stay tuned because their interest has been captured and they want to hear the rest of the news story.

In most news stories, as mentioned, the lead is concerned with some aspect of the who, the what, the when, the where of the H-O-E-O. The first example of a news lead about the robbery is written in a who, what, where, when order. The second illustration of the same robbery story is written in a when, who, what, where order.

As you study additional broadcast news stories and begin writing, you will discover that although the why and the how of an H-O-E-O may be important, it is better in broadcasting to use these two only when they will help you elaborate the details, and even then only when those details are absolutely necessary.

As you listen to the opening of each news story in a news report, note that the lead in each story is most often written as a direct and simple statement of fact. The statement is made to inform the listener-viewer, but at the same time it is written to relate the event to the listener-viewer.

One way to focus that interest in the listener-viewer's mind and emotion is to use the principle of repetition, which is sometimes referred to as purposeful redundancy. This means that repetition is an important part of each news story. As a writing technique it is used to clarify and to gain attention. This technique has been talked about and used deliberately ever since Aristotle made his observations about repetition in an effort to explain how it can be used in the art of persuasion. This occurred about 335 B.C.

Communication research over the years has demonstrated that various forms of repetition are necessary if you are to succeed in catching and holding the listener-viewer's attention.

Several specific techniques and suggestions for developing the use of repetition are described in Chapter 6, "Newswriting Techniques." Also note the use of repetition as a writing technique in Step 2 in the Six-step Process, and in Step 2 in the Seven-step Process. These processes are described and illustrated later in this chapter. You will use them when you begin writing.

One word of caution about the use of repetition. Do not use it just for the sake of repeating. Obviously it should not be shoved into the listener-viewer's ear. Repetition, or purposeful redundancy, should be used primarily for clarifying and for adding needed details. Most of the time you will use different words and different phrases. When you begin writing, each process will help you develop this technique

Purposeful redundancy, or repetition, is used specifically in news reports that are being made at different times of the day. For example, its use is particularly helpful during the six o'clock or six-thirty evening newscasts. News reports at that time have a great deal of competition in most family home environments. The writer's problem is to get individuals to comprehend in spite of all the distractions. There will be plenty of them because this is the first gathering time for most families after a long day that involves school and the problems of making a living. It is also family decision time for settling disputes and determining what various family members will do that evening and the next day.

SELECTING THE NEWS LEAD

The first time a news story is written it is generally specific and direct. Its opening statement, the lead, is referred to in most stations as being a hard news lead. Hard news lead writing as a technique is used by the majority of radio and television stations. The same kind of immediacy is used in leads that update news stories.

The hard news lead is used because it helps keep an updated television story clear, concise, and specific. Radio newswriters also use it to help keep the story clear, concise, and to the point. In general, radio reporting is without elaboration because of the time limit imposed on that medium. The following is an example of hard news writing:

Hard News Lead

> ENVIRONMENTALISTS TURNED DOWN THE USE OF SOFT COAL TO
> REPLACE CLEANER BURNING OIL, TODAY.

When more air-time is available, a more general feature type of lead may be used. Such a lead makes it possible for the writer to be concerned with some of the background details and may sometimes sound as if it were written as a feature story or a commentary. Frequently this kind of lead presents the historical aspects of what is being reported. This type of lead is referred to by most writers as a soft news lead.

Soft News Lead

> ENVIRONMENTALISTS SEEM TO HAVE WON THE FIRST ROUND IN THE
> BATTLE TO REPLACE HIGH-PRICED OIL WITH CHEAP COAL. THEIR VOTE
> TODAY IMPLIES DIRTY AIR IS NOT WORTH MORE HEAT IN THE HOME.

Listen to the morning network television newscasts and you will note how the use of the soft lead permits newswriters to be creative and imaginative.

The Umbrella or Comprehensive News Lead

There are several other news leads that you will learn to use after you become proficient in writing the hard news lead and the soft news lead. One of these is the umbrella or comprehensive news lead. This type of lead is used to introduce several stories that are related. For example, a news outlet may use this lead to report events that have kept the fire department or the police department busy during the day. The umbrella lead is especially useful when no single H-O-E-O is an adequate story by itself. Most of the time the umbrella or comprehensive lead is used to cover events that are closely related. For example:

> RAIN AND FLOODWATERS IN NORTH AMERICA, EUROPE, AND SOUTH
> ASIA ARE IN THE NEWS TONIGHT. IN THE SOUTH CENTRAL UNITED
> STATES A TWO-WEEK DOWN-POUR IS PRODUCING FLOODING RIVERS IN
> ARKANSAS, LOUISIANA, MISSISSIPPI, AND TEXAS. IN WEST GERMANY,
> TORRENTIAL RAINS HAVE PUT THE RHINE RIVER OUT OF ITS BANKS
> FROM DUSSELDORF IN THE NORTH TO THE BLACK FOREST IN THE
> SOUTH. MONSOON WEATHER IN INDIA HAS CAUSED THE MUDDY
> GANGES TO TAKE THE LIVES OF OVER TWO THOUSAND VICTIMS.

The Literary Allusion and Parody News Lead

This news lead parallels a famous saying in literature or a current saying that is well known. The object of this type of lead is to catch and hold the listener-viewer's attention and interest. However, like most things that work well, this lead is generally most effective when not overworked. Here is an example of a literary allusion lead:

> WHEN THE GROUNDHOG CAME OUT OF HIS BURROW TODAY AND SAW
> HIS SHADOW, HE MIGHT HAVE CRIED, "BEWARE THE IDES OF MARCH."
> IF HE HAD, HE WOULD HAVE BEEN WARNING ALL THOSE WITHIN
> SOUND OF HIS VOICE TO EXPECT SIX MORE WEEKS OF WINTER.

The Question News Lead

The question lead is effective on occasion. However, a question, more times than not, invites a negative answer from many listener-viewers. If your listener-viewers can say no to your question, or if the question even calls up a subliminal negative reaction to it, the lead loses its strength as an attention device. When listener-viewers can say no to your question, you turn them off. Therefore, in general, avoid the question lead.

It is true that the question lead may work for some writers the first time. But too frequently its success is misleading—like expecting to be a top reporter after a first lucky break. Here is an example of the question lead:

> WILL YOU FLY FROM THE ATLANTIC TO THE PACIFIC COAST FOR
> NINETY-NINE DOLLARS EACH WAY? TWO MAJOR AIRLINE COMPANIES
> ARE BETTING YOU AND THOUSANDS OF OTHERS WILL DURING
> FEBRUARY AND MARCH. THIS NEW TICKET RATE GOES ON SALE NEXT
> WEEK IN AN EFFORT TO ERASE THE RED INK THAT EMPTY SEATS ARE
> CURRENTLY ACCUMULATING.

FINDING NEWS

Every community has specific events and specific interests that attract the attention of its citizens. That is why many of the H-O-E-Os occurring in a community are more important to the listener-viewers living there than is national and international news.

Naturally the larger the station coverage, whether direct or by cable-vision, the greater will be the number of people who are served. Local news coverage is essential to the total program schedule of most stations. Certainly local reports are a must if merchants in the surrounding towns are to be persuaded to use the radio and television facilities for advertising goods and services.

When a station extends its signal into surrounding communities, the amount of local news reported for each community is generally in direct ratio to the number of listener-viewers and the amount of advertising from each community. Of course what happens in one community is always weighed against the events of every other community being served. This balance is an essential policy that reporters will be asked to observe.

WHAT MAKES NEWS IMPORTANT

News reporting is, therefore, important to radio and television stations whether the news covers social activities, community events, criminal acts, lawsuits, court activities, governmental issues, politics, taxes, or community foibles. Most stations will present as much coverage as they can financially afford because increasing the number of listener-viewers is good broadcast business. However, the primary criteria for determining whether an item is local, regional, national, or international news is the number of people affected and how they respond to each H-O-E-O.

For example, during the 1981 Theodore Bundy murder cases in Florida, the trials were moved from place to place because news coverage was so extensive and interest in the accused's personality so high that the courts were unable to find objective jurors. When the first trial in the series was moved from Tallahassee to Miami, over 500 radio and television news personnel were flown in to cover what originally was thought would be a routine event in a local court. Nevertheless, because of the widespread publicity, this murder case received international as well as national news coverage.

Not long ago what affected the lives of human beings in one community was in general confined to that community. However, with the development of jet air service and communication via satellite, even small community interests may become national or international in scope. The cost of oil in the Middle East increases the price of gas at the local pump. Ordinarily the citizen filling his gas tank would not care about the problems contributing to disruptions occurring in foreign governments. But when a foreign country's disruptions touch the lives and the pocketbooks of other people around the world, the motorist's news horizon is likely to expand. The cost of filling a gas tank becomes a part of both local and international news.

Major financial investments that are far removed from the local scene may take on local meanings. The price of gold or diamonds, or the cost of sporting events, may expand the local horizon. A prize fight in South Africa may create a local demand and as a result the event is televised locally to satisfy a local interest.

Finally, judging whether an H-O-E-O is local, regional, national, or international is determined by how many people are affected and how many people become involved. As a newswriter you need to become aware of these wider implications. Their use may be the criteria by which you can develop a major news story.

USING A PROCESS FOR WRITING NEWS

"How do I begin? What should I write first? How do I put a story together?" These are the three questions most often asked by the beginning radio and television newswriter.

When there is no specific answer, most beginners start by imitating those who are already members of the profession. Imitation, although a deterrent to originality, is a normal human procedure for most beginners in everything. Jokingly we say, "Monkey see, monkey do."

However, using a writing process is an organized approach to developing an ability to write. A process approach can help the beginner discover how to report facts and save learning time.

The two processes in this chapter will help you organize and develop your news story. In fact, you will find that each of these processes is a formulated procedure designed specifically to help you in the same way that a tool serves a specific purpose. Each process is to the writer what a set of wrenches is to a mechanic, what a set of tools is to a carpenter, what a loom is to a weaver, what a palette of colors is to a painter. Each process is a device to help you achieve a better end result, a better news story.

These two processes, the Six-step and the Seven-step, are based on the normal communicating habits of human beings. The steps in each process, while different, are easily followed because they utilize mental and emotional responses that everyone experiences in reacting to visual and verbal stimuli. Specifically, the step-by-step procedure is designed to help you select, from the hundreds of ideas generated by each news H-O-E-O, the specific ones that will be most useful in detailing your news story. Each process step helps do this by indicating what to include and how to do it. By following the process step by step, you will learn how to write. As a result, writing will become a pleasure because you will be able to produce a message that communicates efficiently and effectively, thus fulfilling your responsibility to the listener-viewer.

WRITING A NEWS STORY

There are two basic procedures to be performed before you begin writing. The first is collecting the needed information. The second is organizing that information. After you have gained experience in writing you may be able to perform these two basic steps simultaneously. For example, while you are collecting the facts about an H-O-E-O, your knowledge and familiarity with the writing process will help you decide where each bit of information fits best.

Collecting Information

After you have become a reporter, you may go to the source so you can see what's taking place and ask questions. On other occasions you will use the telephone and talk with witnesses. Other times you will get your facts from a wire service. For now, let us begin with a simple news source. Its use will save you time and speed up your class work.

Suppose for this first story we select a newspaper account of an earthquake that occurred in South America.

Organizing Information

As you read the newspaper clipping you follow the same procedure you would if you were a full-fledged reporter. You organize the information available into a *fact sheet*. A fact sheet is a series of statements about an H-O-E-O. These statements are generally listed in the order of their importance. The fact sheet concerning the earthquake story has its facts listed as follows:

1. An earthquake occurred sometime late yesterday in Lima, Peru, South America.
2. The quake registered a peak of seven on the Mercali scale of 12.
3. The reading of seven makes it the strongest earthquake to have hit that area.
4. Thousands of people have been left homeless. No detailed information is available.
5. The city of Lima is said to be in ruins.
6. Twenty-one deaths have been reported. No official report of the number of injuries.
7. Lima police report 14 of the dead were in one church.
8. United States Red Cross workers are being sent to the area.
9. The United Nations may declare Lima a disaster area.
10. The information source is the Associated Press.

Now that you have these facts, you need to begin examining the information in terms of how to write it. Let us begin by using the Six-step Process. This means you will select information from these facts that will fulfill the function of each step in this process. To help you do this it is well to memorize the format of the process. You should also prepare a condensed version of it on a 3-×-5 card and keep it handy as a ready reference. The following is the information with which you need to be familiar in order to use the Six-step Process in learning how to write.

THE SIX-STEP PROCESS AND NEWSWRITING

Step 1. Initial Statement   The initial statement is the lead. Writing the lead was discussed earlier. You will recall that by the very nature of a news story the lead gives the listener-viewer a concept of what the news story is all about. Therefore the lead, especially the first few words, must be stated in such a way that it will catch the listener-viewer's attention. While the writer cannot say, "Hey! Did you hear about the earthquake!", the attention part of the lead does serve that purpose. The lead can best do this by beginning with what are called "throwaway words." These are used before the writer states or implies a thesis, theme, or central idea as it relates to a problem, need, feeling, conflict, or desire. Stating the thesis, theme, or central idea is necessary because the development of the entire story depends on it.

Step 2. Repetition and Reinforcement Statement   The content of this step repeats in different words the concept stated or implied in the lead statement. Step 2 specifically helps the listener-viewer learn more and want to hear more about how the problem, need, feeling, conflict, or desire is to be considered or resolved in the rest of the story. The specific use of repetition, or purposeful redundancy, and its need was discussed earlier.

Step 3. Transitional Statement   The content of this step is based on Steps 1 and 2. While Step 3 is basically a transitional statement, it also prepares the listener-viewer to accept a fuller explanation and elaboration of the lead's thesis, theme, or central idea as it relates to a problem, need, feeling, or desire. The transitional statement is placed here in the story to heighten the listener-viewer's interest in what is to come. At the same time it helps avoid an abrupt shift into the details of the story.

Step 4. Visualization Statement   The content of this step states or gives such details as are needed to help the listener-viewer visualize the thesis, theme, or central idea and its relationship to a specific problem, need, feeling, or desire. In this way Step 4 gives the listener-viewer a better understanding of what is happening or taking place, and creates an interest in hearing how this relationship can be resolved.

Step 5. Satisfaction Statement   The content and details of this step help the listener-viewer experience the satisfaction of understanding the concept stated in Step 1 before you conclude your story in Step 6.

Step 6. Action or Result Statement   This final step must state or suggest the final action that is to be taken or that should be made with regard to the lead statement in Step 1. In other words, Step 6 is the conclusion of your story.

Now that you have the need, reason, and purpose for each step in mind, you are ready to follow the writing of a story about the Lima earthquake. Doing so will help you visualize and experience how each step contributes to the development of a news story. First we look at Step 1 and begin thinking in terms of a lead. We discovered previously that a lead must be based on a specific aspect of the total information available. To help clarify this concept, think in terms of the 5 Ws and H, the who, what, when, where, why, and how about the earthquake in Lima, Peru.

As we begin reading through the fact sheet data, we realize that the lead must be stated so it will catch the listener-viewer's attention and convince him that what is being reported is of such importance, either directly or indirectly, that the entire story is worth hearing. Keep in mind too that the lead must lend itself to further development in the remaining five steps. On occasion you may need to write two or three leads and select the one that is most appropriate, or perhaps combine parts of each lead into one.

Sometimes stating the source of your information first helps get the listener-viewer's attention. After thinking the problem through, suppose we identify Step 1 and write:

STEP 1—INITIAL STATEMENT, THESIS, THEME, CENTRAL IDEA, ETC.:
THE ASSOCIATED PRESS REPORTS AN EARTHQUAKE STRUCK LIMA, PERU, LATE YESTERDAY.

We read this lead and note that it is a statement of fact. It tells what happened and where it happened. Although we may change it, for the present the statement seems to fulfill the function required of a lead because: (1) it is a clear statement of a thesis, theme, or central idea that relates to a problem, need, feeling, or desire; (2) it is a statement that lends itself to further development; (3) it is a statement that catches the listener-viewer's attention.

Before going on to Step 2 in the Six-step Process we reread the fact sheet. While doing this we discover what we should say in Step 2 in order to repeat and reinforce the thesis, theme, or central idea stated or implied in the lead. Naturally, although we repeat, we will use different words. It is necessary to repeat our initial statement because repetition is an essential aspect of broadcast news communicating.

With the definition of Step 2 in mind, a need to reinforce through repetition, we look over the Lima, Peru, fact sheet and write:

STEP 2—REPETITION-REINFORCEMENT STATEMENT:
THE QUAKE IS CONSIDERED TO BE THE WORST EVER TO HIT THE LIMA AREA.

After rereading Step 1, the lead, and what we have just written for Step 2, we turn to Step 3.

By definition Step 3 must be transitional in purpose. Furthermore, Step 3 must help the story flow from Step 2 to Step 4. Therefore Step 3 may be a continuation, a slight reiteration, or a statement in different words about what is stated in Steps 1 and 2. According to the intent of quality newswriting, Step 3 must increase interest in the story and prepare the listener-viewer for a fuller understanding. First we reread what we have written for Steps 1 and 2:

THE ASSOCIATED PRESS REPORTS AN EARTHQUAKE STRUCK LIMA, PERU, LATE YESTERDAY. THE QUAKE IS CONSIDERED TO BE THE WORST EVER TO HIT THE LIMA AREA.

Then we review the fact sheet data and write the following:

STEP 3—TRANSITIONAL STATEMENT:
TWENTY-ONE DEATHS HAVE BEEN REPORTED SO FAR, WITH NO OFFICIAL COUNT OF THE NUMBER OF INJURIES.

As we reread what we have just written we note that it is factual, in keeping with the lead, and as a transitional statement it continues to create interest in the earthquake as a disaster. Furthermore, we have the listener-viewer ready to hear more details. The question now is, what should we write for Step 4? What facts do we have that best lend themselves to helping the listener-viewer visualize what is happening in Lima, Peru?

The definition of Step 4 states that we should list or describe details about what is happening. For this story we need to supply the listener-viewer with specific facts about the earthquake. The details we have are skimpy, but we will do our best by visualizing what has actually occurred. In other words, what we say in Step 4 should help the listener-viewer create mental images of what is happening to the people in the quake area. Naturally, our visualization statement should also create a desire to hear more.

After reviewing the fact sheet data, we reread what we have written:

THE ASSOCIATED PRESS REPORTS AN EARTHQUAKE STRUCK LIMA, PERU, LATE YESTERDAY. THE QUAKE IS CONSIDERED TO BE THE WORST EVER TO HIT THE LIMA AREA. TWENTY-ONE DEATHS HAVE BEEN REPORTED SO FAR, WITH NO OFFICIAL COUNT OF THE NUMBER OF INJURIES.

We decide to fulfill Step 4's function by writing:

STEP 4—VISUALIZATION STATEMENT:
POLICE IN LIMA REPORT 14 OF THE DEAD WERE FOUND IN THE RUBBLE OF ONE COLLAPSED CHURCH.

Again we read all we have written and decide that additional details are needed for Step 5, the satisfaction statement. The definition of this step says that what we write should help the listener-viewer gain satisfaction from understanding what has happened, what is happening, and what may happen.

After reviewing the remaining details in the fact sheet, we reread what we have written:

THE ASSOCIATED PRESS REPORTS AN EARTHQUAKE STRUCK LIMA, PERU, LATE YESTERDAY. THE QUAKE IS CONSIDERED TO BE THE WORST EVER TO HIT THE LIMA AREA. TWENTY-ONE DEATHS HAVE BEEN REPORTED SO FAR, WITH NO OFFICIAL COUNT OF THE NUMBER OF INJURIES. POLICE IN LIMA REPORT 14 OF THE DEAD WERE FOUND IN THE RUBBLE OF ONE COLLAPSED CHURCH.

For Step 5 we write as follows:

STEP 5—SATISFACTION STATEMENT:
THE QUAKE, WITH A PEAK OF SEVEN ON THE MERCALI SCALE OF TWELVE, LEFT THOUSANDS HOMELESS AND THE CITY OF LIMA IN RUINS.

We reread that statement and conclude that it should satisfy the interest and curiosity of the majority of listener-viewers by letting them know just how bad the quake really is.

We look over our fact sheet and note that we have used almost all the information available to us. We therefore turn to the definition of Step 6, the action, result, or conclusion statement.

The definition of this step says that the purpose of Step 6 is to come to a satisfactory story conclusion. To do this, we note, we should suggest the actions that are being taken, or are expected to be taken, about the quake. Such a statement will help answer the listener-viewer's questions and interest in what is being done about this disaster. To help us get a feeling for writing such a final statement we reread what we have written:

THE ASSOCIATED PRESS REPORTS AN EARTHQUAKE STRUCK LIMA, PERU, LATE YESTERDAY. THE QUAKE IS CONSIDERED TO BE THE WORST EVER TO HIT THE LIMA AREA. TWENTY-ONE DEATHS HAVE BEEN REPORTED SO FAR, WITH NO OFFICIAL COUNT OF THE NUMBER OF INJURIES. POLICE IN LIMA REPORT 14 OF THE DEAD WERE FOUND IN THE RUBBLE OF ONE COLLAPSED CHURCH. THE QUAKE, WITH A PEAK OF SEVEN ON THE MERCALI SCALE OF TWELVE, LEFT THOUSANDS HOMELESS AND THE CITY OF LIMA IN RUINS.

We look over what information is left in our fact sheet and write:

UNITED STATES RED CROSS WORKERS WITH SUPPLIES ARE BEING
RUSHED TO THE STRICKEN AREA. THE UNITED NATIONS IS EXPECTED
TO DECLARE LIMA A DISASTER AREA.

Now we go back and read aloud what we have written in its entirety.
If there are inconsistencies or errors, we make such corrections as are
necessary. After we have read, and rewritten if necessary, we type out a
copy. Because we are concerned here with learning how to write, the
following format is adequate at this time. The Lima, Peru, earthquake story
is strictly factual and is, therefore, hard news.

THE ASSOCIATED PRESS REPORTS AN EARTHQUAKE STRUCK LIMA,
PERU, LATE YESTERDAY. THE QUAKE IS CONSIDERED TO BE THE
WORST EVER TO HIT THE LIMA AREA. TWENTY-ONE DEATHS HAVE
BEEN REPORTED SO FAR, WITH NO OFFICIAL COUNT OF THE NUMBER
OF INJURIES. POLICE IN LIMA REPORT 14 OF THE DEAD WERE FOUND IN
THE RUBBLE OF ONE COLLAPSED CHURCH. THE QUAKE, WITH A PEAK
OF SEVEN ON THE MERCALI SCALE OF TWELVE, LEFT THOUSANDS
HOMELESS AND THE CITY OF LIMA IN RUINS. UNITED STATES RED
CROSS WORKERS WITH SUPPLIES ARE BEING RUSHED TO THE STRICKEN
AREA. THE UNITED NATIONS IS EXPECTED TO DECLARE LIMA A
DISASTER AREA.

Examples of Six-step Process News Stories:

Review the definition for each step before you read each example.

Example 1

STEP 1—INITIAL STATEMENT:
MORE THAN 170 INDONESIANS DROWNED IN 30-FOOT TIDAL WAVES
THAT SMASHED INTO THE ISLAND OF LOMBLEN, SATURDAY NIGHT.

STEP 2—REPETITION-REINFORCEMENT STATEMENT:
OFFICIALS SAID THE WAVES, MOVING AT MORE THAN 90-MILES AN
HOUR, CRASHED DOWN ON FOUR VILLAGES.

STEP 3—TRANSITIONAL STATEMENT:
ONLY 23 SURVIVORS, ALL SERIOUSLY INJURED, WERE RESCUED FROM
THE ISLAND.

STEP 4—VISUALIZATION STATEMENT:
THE GIANT WAVES WERE BELIEVED TO HAVE BEEN CAUSED BY THE
COLLAPSE OF THE THREE-THOUSAND-FOOT GUNUNG WERNUNG
VOLCANO INTO THE FORBES SEA.

STEP 5—SATISFACTION STATEMENT:
THE SWIFT-MOVING WAVES CRESTED AT 30-FEET AND PLUNGED DOWN
ON THE INHABITANTS AS THEY SLEPT.

STEP 6—ACTION, RESULT, CONCLUSION STATEMENT:
SO FAR 171 BODIES HAVE BEEN RECOVERED FROM BENEATH TONS OF
SAND AND MUD HURLED ASHORE BY THE GIANT WAVES. SEVEN
HUNDRED PERSONS ARE STILL MISSING.

Now the story in its entirety.

MORE THAN 170 INDONESIANS DROWNED IN 30-FOOT TIDAL WAVES
THAT SMASHED INTO THE ISLAND OF LOMBLEN, SATURDAY NIGHT. THE
WAVES, MOVING AT MORE THAN 90-MILES AN HOUR, CRASHED DOWN
ON FOUR VILLAGES. ONLY 23 SURVIVORS, ALL SERIOUSLY INJURED,
WERE RESCUED FROM THE ISLAND. THE GIANT WAVES WERE
BELIEVED TO HAVE BEEN CAUSED BY THE COLLAPSE OF THE THREE-
THOUSAND-FOOT GUNUNG WERNUNG VOLCANO INTO THE FORBES SEA.
THE SWIFT-MOVING WAVES CRESTED AT 30-FEET AND PLUNGED DOWN
ON THE INHABITANTS AS THEY SLEPT. SO FAR, 171 BODIES HAVE BEEN
RECOVERED FROM BENEATH TONS OF SAND AND MUD HURLED
ASHORE BY THE GIANT WAVES. SEVEN HUNDRED PERSONS ARE STILL
MISSING.

Example 2

The following is a hard news lead local television story given by an anchor
person. Note how the entire story is factual.

STEP 1—INITIAL STATEMENT:
GENERAL MOTORS IS RECALLING ALMOST 500-THOUSAND LATE MODEL
STATION WAGONS.

STEP 2—REPETITION-REINFORCEMENT STATEMENT:
A G-M SPOKESMAN SAID THAT ALL 1977, 78 AND 79 CHEVROLET,
PONTIAC, OLDSMOBILE, AND BUICK FULL-SIZED STATION WAGONS WERE
BEING RECALLED.

STEP 3—TRANSITIONAL STATEMENT:
THE PURPOSE OF THE RECALL IS TO REPLACE THE LATCHES ON REAR-STORAGE COMPARTMENTS IN THE STATION WAGONS.

STEP 4—VISUALIZATION STATEMENT:
G-M HAS RECEIVED THREE REPORTS OF CHILDREN TRAPPED IN THE COMPARTMENTS AND ONE OF THE CHILDREN DIED.

STEP 5—SATISFACTION STATEMENT:
THE NEW LATCHES WILL PREVENT SMALL CHILDREN FROM CLIMBING IN AND BECOMING TRAPPED.

STEP 6—ACTION, RESULT, CONCLUSION STATEMENT:
THE NEW LATCHES ARE BEING REPLACED FREE.

Now the story without the steps indicated:

GENERAL MOTORS IS RECALLING ALMOST 500-THOUSAND LATE MODEL STATION WAGONS. A G-M SPOKESMAN SAID THAT ALL 1977, 78, AND 79 CHEVROLET, PONTIAC, OLDSMOBILE, AND BUICK FULL-SIZED STATION WAGONS WERE BEING RECALLED. THE PURPOSE OF THE RECALL IS TO REPLACE THE LATCHES ON REAR-STORAGE COMPARTMENTS IN THE STATION WAGONS. G-M HAS RECEIVED THREE REPORTS OF CHILDREN TRAPPED IN THE COMPARTMENTS AND ONE OF THE CHILDREN DIED. THE NEW LATCHES WILL PREVENT SMALL CHILDREN FROM CLIMBING IN AND BECOMING TRAPPED. THE NEW LATCHES ARE BEING REPLACED FREE.

Six-step Process Soft News Lead Stories

Hard news leads are relatively easy to write. Doing so requires the use of facts plus organization and arrangement of these facts. Soft news leads, as noted, may be used to help establish mood, feelings, attitudes, or reactions. Therefore when an H-O-E-O seems important to a station's listener-viewers, but does not lend itself to the hard news lead format, it may be more effective if written as soft news. The following television news story is an example. Note how Steps 2 and 3 grow out of Step 1, a soft lead, which is almost commentary.

STEP 1—INITIAL STATEMENT:
CONSUMERS RECEIVED SOME DEPRESSING NEWS TODAY.

STEP 2—REPETITION-REINFORCEMENT STATEMENT:
INFLATION IS REPORTED TO HAVE REACHED A DREADED MILESTONE.

STEP 3—TRANSITIONAL STATEMENT:
FOR THE FIRST TIME SINCE 1967, PRICES HAVE DOUBLED.

STEP 4—VISUALIZATION STATEMENT:
THE UNITED STATES LABOR DEPARTMENT REPORTED THAT THE
CONSUMER PRICE INDEX HAS PASSED THE 200-MARK.

STEP 5—SATISFACTION STATEMENT:
INFLATION INCREASES HAVE CAUSED THE AVERAGE WORKER'S
PURCHASING POWER TO DROP AN ADDITIONAL THREE-POINT-SIX
PERCENT.

STEP 6—ACTION, RESULT, CONCLUSION STATEMENT:
THIS MEANS THAT WHAT A CONSUMER PAID 100-DOLLARS FOR IN 1967
WILL COST HIM 200-DOLLARS TODAY.

Here is the story without the steps indicated.

CONSUMERS RECEIVED SOME DEPRESSING NEWS TODAY. INFLATION IS
REPORTED TO HAVE REACHED A DREADED MILESTONE. FOR THE
FIRST TIME SINCE 1967, PRICES HAVE DOUBLED. THE UNITED STATES
LABOR DEPARTMENT REPORTED THAT THE CONSUMER PRICE INDEX
HAS PASSED THE 200 MARK. INFLATION INCREASES HAVE CAUSED THE
AVERAGE WORKER'S PURCHASING POWER TO DROP AN ADDITIONAL
THREE-POINT-SIX PERCENT. THIS MEANS THAT WHAT A CONSUMER
PAID 100-DOLLARS FOR IN 1967 WILL COST HIM 200-DOLLARS TODAY.

It was pointed out during the initial explanation of a soft news lead
that it is quite as specific or as factual as is the hard news lead. Sometimes
a phrase, a clause, or an additional idea may be added to help it be more
specific. When this occurs, the lead and story may become a kind of
combination of soft and hard. Such a television news story may be written
as follows:

STEP 1—INITIAL STATEMENT:
PRESIDENT CARTER, IN A LOW KEY CEREMONY,

STEP 2—REPETITION-REINFORCEMENT STATEMENT:
ANNOUNCED HE WILL SEEK ANOTHER FOUR YEARS IN THE WHITE
HOUSE

STEP 3—TRANSITIONAL STATEMENT:
WITH VICE PRESIDENT MONDALE AS HIS RUNNING MATE.

STEP 4—VISUALIZATION STATEMENT:

CALLING IT A SOMBER TIME, THE PRESIDENT SAID THE IRANIAN CRISIS DEMANDS HIS CLOSEST ATTENTION AND HE THEREFORE WILL CURTAIL HIS POLITICAL ACTIVITIES FOR THE NEXT MONTH.

STEP 5—SATISFACTION STATEMENT:

THE PRESIDENT ALSO NOTED HE WOULD HAVE PREFERRED TO POSTPONE THE ANNOUNCEMENT, BUT ELECTION LAWS REQUIRE A FORMAL DECLARATION.

STEP 6—ACTION, RESULT, CONCLUSION STATEMENT:

SINCE HE HAS BEEN PRESIDENT, HE POINTED OUT, HE HAS MADE SOME HARD DECISIONS, AND HE EXPECTS TO MAKE OTHERS.

Here is the story without the steps indicated.

PRESIDENT CARTER, IN A LOW KEY CEREMONY, ANNOUNCED HE WILL SEEK ANOTHER FOUR YEARS IN THE WHITE HOUSE WITH VICE PRESIDENT MONDALE AS HIS RUNNING MATE. CALLING IT A SOMBER TIME, THE PRESIDENT SAID THE IRANIAN CRISIS DEMANDS HIS CLOSEST ATTENTION AND HE THEREFORE WILL CURTAIL HIS POLITICAL ACTIVITIES FOR THE NEXT MONTH. THE PRESIDENT ALSO NOTED HE WOULD HAVE PREFERRED TO POSTPONE THE ANNOUNCEMENT, BUT ELECTION LAWS REQUIRE A FORMAL DECLARATION. SINCE HE HAS BEEN PRESIDENT, HE POINTED OUT, HE HAS MADE SOME HARD DECISIONS, AND HE EXPECTS TO MAKE OTHERS.

The following Six-step Process news story has a typical soft news lead.

STEP 1—INITIAL STATEMENT:

THERE MUST BE A WAY TO TEACH A DOG NOT TO KILL CATS. THE METHOD USED BY JACK HORNER OF PANCAKE, TEXAS, MAY BE THE WRONG ONE.

STEP 2—REPETITION-REINFORCEMENT STATEMENT:

AT LEAST JACK'S METHOD IS WRONG IF YOU WANT TO STAY OUT OF JAIL.

STEP 3—TRANSITIONAL STATEMENT:

HORNER WAS ARRESTED BY THE DEAF SMITH COUNTY SHERIFF MONDAY, AFTER A NEIGHBOR REPORTED A DEAD CAT TIED AROUND THE NECK OF HORNER'S DOG.

STEP 4— VISUALIZATION STATEMENT:
HORNER IS AN ENVIRONMENTALIST AND THE AUTHOR OF A BOOK ON
JACK RABBITS. HE WAS RECENTLY A GUEST ON THE "TODAY" SHOW TO
DEFEND ENVIRONMENTAL CAUSES.

STEP 5—SATISFACTION STATEMENT:
HE DENIES THE CHARGE OF CRUELTY TO ANIMALS.

STEP 6—ACTION, RESULT, CONCLUSION STATEMENT:
HORNER SAYS HE'S BEING HARASSED BECAUSE OF HIS RECENT
OPPOSITION TO THE CONSTRUCTION OF A DOGFOOD FACTORY IN
PANCAKE.

Here is the story without the steps indicated.

THERE MUST BE A WAY TO TEACH A DOG NOT TO KILL CATS.
THE METHOD USED BY JACK HORNER OF PANCAKE, TEXAS, MAY BE THE
WRONG ONE. AT LEAST JACK'S METHOD IS WRONG IF YOU WANT TO STAY
OUT OF JAIL. HORNER WAS ARRESTED BY THE DEAF SMITH COUNTY
SHERIFF MONDAY, AFTER A NEIGHBOR REPORTED A DEAD CAT
TIED AROUND THE NECK OF HORNER'S DOG. HORNER IS AN
ENVIRONMENTALIST AND THE AUTHOR OF A BOOK ON JACK RABBITS.
HE WAS RECENTLY A GUEST ON THE "TODAY" SHOW TO DEFEND
ENVIRONMENTAL CAUSES. HE DENIES THE CHARGE OF CRUELTY TO
ANIMALS. HORNER SAYS HE'S BEING HARASSED BECAUSE OF HIS
RECENT OPPOSITION TO THE CONSTRUCTION OF A DOGFOOD FACTORY
IN PANCAKE.

ASSIGNMENTS: WRITING THE SIX-STEP NEWS STORY

1. Use a newspaper or newspaper wire service as a news source.
2. Select and clip a story from your source for each of the following types of stories: local, state, regional, national, international.
3. Mount each story-clipping on an $8\frac{1}{2}$-×-11-inch sheet of typing paper. Be sure the sheet is identified with your name, class, date, and the nature of the specific assignment.
4. From each clipping work out a detailed fact sheet. You will write your story from this fact sheet. Think of it as being the equivalent of a fact sheet you would work out as a practicing reporter. *Be sure to avoid using the original writer's phrases and descriptions.*
5. Select fact sheets from the five types of stories and write as many of the following leads—hard news lead, soft news lead, literary allusion

or parody lead, and question lead—as your instructor assigns. Naturally, the more you write the better writer you will become.

6. Now you are ready to begin writing news stories. If the leads you have written are adequate, use them. If not, write new ones. Be sure to identify each step as you write. Follow the form used in the explanatory illustrations. For example, Step 1—Initial Statement, Thesis, Theme, Central Idea. Then type in your lead and go on to Steps 2, 3, and so on until you complete each step in the Six-step Process. Your instructor will assign the number of stories you are to write.

Note: Following the step-by-step process is a routine that will help you develop an intuitive feeling for writing.

7. After you complete each story step-by-step, be sure to type a double-spaced copy for each story on a separate page. Your instructor may want you to follow a special format.

Remember, routine repetition is the fastest way to learn if it is disciplined repetition. Each learning routine should be carried out as efficiently and as rapidly as possible until it becomes a habit. This is what you did when you learned to drive a car or swing a tennis racket. You can learn to write the same way.

8. When you turn in an assignment, remember that your instructor will probably need: a copy of your news source; a copy of your fact sheet; a step-by-step copy of your written news story; a copy of your story in its entirety. Each page you turn in should be adequately identified.

Modifying the Six-step Newswriting Process

On occasion the available time on a newscast must be changed. When this occurs your news story will need to be shortened; all you need to do is remove one or more of its steps. The following is an example of how the Six-step Process news story may be modified for radio or television. For the complete story, see the version that was used earlier in this chapter.

STEP 1—INITIAL STATEMENT:
CONSUMERS RECEIVED SOME DEPRESSING NEWS TODAY.

STEP 2—REPETITION-REINFORCEMENT STATEMENT:
INFLATION IS REPORTED TO HAVE REACHED A DREADED MILESTONE.

STEP 3—TRANSITIONAL STATEMENT:
FOR THE FIRST TIME SINCE 1967, PRICES HAVE DOUBLED.

STEP 6—ACTION, RESULT, CONCLUSION STATEMENT:
THIS MEANS THAT WHAT A CONSUMER PAID 100-DOLLARS FOR IN 1967
COSTS HIM 200-DOLLARS TODAY.

Here is the shortened story in its entirety.

CONSUMERS RECEIVED SOME DEPRESSING NEWS TODAY. INFLATION IS
REPORTED TO HAVE REACHED A DREADED MILESTONE. FOR THE
FIRST TIME SINCE 1967, PRICES HAVE DOUBLED. THIS MEANS THAT
WHAT A CONSUMER PAID 100-DOLLARS FOR IN 1967 COSTS HIM
200-DOLLARS TODAY.

Steps 4 and 5 in the original story have been omitted. Step 2 seems to be needed to focus the listener-viewer's attention on the main point of the story. Read the modified story with and without Step 2 and you will see how the story is stronger when it is retained.

Assignment suggestion: Modify the stories you have written. Think of their being used in a short newscast. You will note that on occasion you will need to change some of the wording.

THE SEVEN-STEP PROCESS AND NEWSWRITING

For some types of H-O-E-Os, a different approach to writing will turn each one into a different type of news story. As you gain experience and expertise in putting language together, you will find some ideas fit the Seven-step Process better than they do the Six-step Process. Later, after you have mastered the Seven-step Process, you will find it may also be modified, and in fact it may even become your favorite approach to writing a news story. For now, however, use it in its complete form even though you may have problems developing Steps 5 and 6. Doing so will give you a broader understanding of how a news story can be developed.

The basic differences between the Six-step and the Seven-step Processes and their use are determined by:

1. The nature and the details of your facts.
2. The point of view you choose for the story. This is always reflected in Step 1, the lead.
3. The writing style selected for developing the news story.
4. The Seven-step Process accommodates the soft lead approach better than the Six-step Process.
5. The writer has more options and can go into greater detail when the need arises.

To understand the Seven-step Process and how to use it, write a news story based on the following fact sheet:

1. Market reports indicate that the large, so-called luxury American automobile isn't selling well on today's market.

2. Many drivers of the large automobile report it has become a liability because of the amount of gas it consumes.

3. Car dealers are admitting that the luxury car is not selling.

4. Owning a luxury car is expensive. It also uses more oil and gas.

5. Manufacturers use more materials in building the luxury car. More powerful engines are needed so there is a total of more weight.

6. Compact cars are selling well, especially foreign makes and models.

7. The increased cost of oil from the Arab nations is affecting buyers and manufacturers alike.

8. Car salesmen are having trouble convincing buyers of the superiority of the luxury car over compact and foreign cars. One driver said, "The symbol of luxury in automobiles today belongs to the car that costs less because it saves gas, not uses it."

9. The foreign car that gets good mileage seems to be the favorite with buyers today.

Before we can write a Seven-step Process news story we must learn what each step should contribute to the story. Let us study the following step definitions and prepare a ready-reference outline on a 3-×-5 card.

Step 1—Initial Statement, the Lead   The initial statement, the lead for the Seven-step Process, should state or imply a thesis, theme, or central idea as it relates to a problem, need, feeling, or desire. While the need for a lead is universal, and therefore similar in these two processes, after the first two steps in the seven-step, the news story is developed differently.

Step 2—Repeats the Step 1 Statement in Different Words   This step should function similarly to Step 2 in the Six-step Process. It should specifically employ the use of repetition and redundancy to catch the listener-viewer's interest.

Step 3—Gives Details or Examples to Illustrate Step 1   This step is in part transitional but its primary purpose is to give information that will illustrate the lead statement in Step 1.

Step 4—Assigns the Origin or Cause of Step 1   This step explains why the situation responsible for the main idea in the lead occurred or came to be.

Step 5—Compares a Similar Idea or Phenomenon with Step 1   This step is self-explanatory in that the writer compares a similar idea with the concept or problem stated in the lead. This comparison helps make what is being talked about clearer to each listener-viewer's frame-of-reference.

Step 6—Contrasts a Dissimilar Idea or Phenomenon with Step 1 In this step the writer is contrasting instead of comparing as in Step 5. It is done, however, for the same reason and purpose, to help the listener-viewer understand.

Step 7—States or Prognosticates the Results or Conclusion This step is the conclusion of the news story. It should be written in a manner that will fulfill the lead's statement in Step 1.

After reviewing the information in the fact sheet about the so-called American luxury car, we begin our news story by writing a soft lead. We must keep in mind that what we say in each succeeding step of this story is determined by what we have said in the lead. Here is one lead and story example. Should you write a story it might be quite different.

STEP 1—INITIAL STATEMENT, THE LEAD:
THE LARGE AMERICAN CAR IS LOSING ITS STATUS AS A SYMBOL OF LUXURY.

STEP 2—REPEATS THE LEAD CONCEPT IN DIFFERENT WORDS:
REPORTS SHOW THAT MOST BUYERS ARE LEAVING THEM IN THE SHOWROOM.

STEP 3—GIVES DETAILS OR EXAMPLES TO ILLUSTRATE STEP 1:
ITS LARGE ENGINE AND HEAVY BODY ARE PUTTING DRIVERS BEHIND THE WHEEL OF SMALLER MODELS.

STEP 4—ASSIGNS THE ORIGIN OR CAUSE OF STEP 1 STATEMENT:
IT IS THE HIGH COST OF MANUFACTURING AND DRIVING THAT IS CAUSING THIS SHIFT IN AUTOMOBILE STATUS.

STEP 5—COMPARES A SIMILAR IDEA OR PHENOMENON WITH STEP 1:
THE NEW CONCEPT IN CAR LUXURY DEFINITELY FAVORS THE CAR WITH A SMALLER APPETITE FOR GAS.

STEP 6—CONTRASTS A DISSIMILAR IDEA OR PHENOMENON WITH STEP 1:
AND THE COMPACT AND THE FOREIGN MODELS ARE OFFERING THE AMERICAN DRIVER JUST THAT.

STEP 7—STATES OR PROGNOSTICATES THE RESULTS OR CONCLUSION:
AS ONE DRIVER PUT IT, THE SYMBOL OF LUXURY IN AUTOMOBILES TODAY BELONGS TO THE CAR THAT COSTS LESS AND SAVES GAS, NOT USES IT.

Here is the story without the steps indicated.

THE LARGE AMERICAN CAR IS LOSING ITS STATUS AS A SYMBOL OF
LUXURY. REPORTS SHOW THAT MOST BUYERS ARE LEAVING THEM IN
THE SHOWROOM. ITS LARGE ENGINE AND HEAVY BODY ARE PUTTING
DRIVERS BEHIND THE WHEEL OF SMALLER MODELS. IT IS THE HIGH
COST OF MANUFACTURING AND DRIVING THAT IS CAUSING THIS SHIFT
IN AUTOMOBILE STATUS. THE NEW CONCEPT IN CAR LUXURY
DEFINITELY FAVORS THE CAR WITH A SMALLER APPETITE FOR GAS.
AND THE COMPACT AND THE FOREIGN MODELS ARE OFFERING THE
AMERICAN DRIVER JUST THAT. AS ONE DRIVER PUT IT, THE SYMBOL
OF LUXURY IN AUTOMOBILES TODAY BELONGS TO THE CAR THAT
COSTS LESS AND SAVES GAS, NOT USES IT.

One of the following seven-step television news stories begins with a
soft lead and one begins with a hard lead. Note how each story develops.

Example 1

STEP 1—INITIAL STATEMENT, THE LEAD:
THEY DON'T WANT THEM, THEY DON'T NEED THEM, THEY'RE NOT
ENTITLED TO THEM. SO, THEY KEEP SENDING THEM BACK.

STEP 2—REPEATS THE LEAD STATEMENT IN DIFFERENT WORDS:
THEM IS A MONTHLY SOCIAL SECURITY CHECK, AND *THEY* ARE ORVAL
AND HELEN SMITH OF DENVER.

STEP 3—GIVES DETAILS OR EXAMPLES TO ILLUSTRATE STEP 1:
THE CHECKS HAVE BEEN COMING MONTHLY FOR THE PAST FOUR
YEARS. AND FOR FOUR YEARS THE SMITHS HAVE BEEN RETURNING
THEM.

STEP 4—ASSIGNS THE ORIGIN OR CAUSE OF STEP 1 STATEMENT:
EVEN THOUGH ORVAL SMITH IS 69-YEARS OLD, HE IS NOT ELIGIBLE
FOR THE CHECKS THAT COME EACH MONTH BECAUSE HE IS STILL
EMPLOYED. HE IS A PHOTOCOPIER FOR I-B-M AND MAKES 20-THOUSAND
DOLLARS A YEAR.

STEP 5—COMPARES SIMILAR IDEAS OR PHENOMENA WITH STEP 1:
UNDER THE LAW SMITH IS ENTITLED TO THE SOCIAL SECURITY CHECKS
LIKE ANY OTHER CITIZEN HIS AGE, PROVIDED HE MAKES NO MORE
THAN THREE-THOUSAND DOLLARS A YEAR.

THE SMITHS HAVE MADE REPEATED CALLS TO THE SOCIAL SECURITY
ADMINISTRATION IN AN EFFORT TO GET THE CHECKS STOPPED. THEY
ARE WORRIED THAT WHEN ORVAL DOES RETIRE, HE MIGHT HAVE
TROUBLE COLLECTING THE MONEY THAT WILL BE DUE HIM.

STEP 7—STATES OR PROGNOSTICATES THE RESULTS OR CONCLUSION:
THE SMITHS BELIEVE THE GOVERNMENT CONTINUES TO SEND THE
CHECKS BECAUSE OF A COMPUTER MALFUNCTION. ORVAL SMITH
APPLIED FOR MEDICARE, WHICH HE DID NOT WANT BUT WAS
ENTITLED TO, ON HIS SIXTY-FIFTH BIRTHDAY. THAT WAS A MISTAKE,
SAYS SMITH. EVIDENTLY THE COMPUTER ALSO ENROLLED HIM IN
SOCIAL SECURITY RETIREMENT BENEFITS.

The story without the steps reads as follows.

THEY DON'T WANT THEM, THEY DON'T NEED THEM, THEY'RE NOT
ENTITLED TO THEM. SO, THEY KEEP SENDING THEM BACK. *THEM* IS A
MONTHLY SOCIAL SECURITY CHECK, AND *THEY* ARE ORVAL AND
HELEN SMITH OF DENVER. THE CHECKS HAVE BEEN COMING MONTHLY
FOR THE PAST FOUR YEARS. AND FOR FOUR YEARS THE SMITHS HAVE
BEEN RETURNING THEM. EVEN THOUGH ORVAL SMITH IS 69-YEARS
OLD, HE IS NOT ELIGIBLE FOR THE CHECKS THAT COME EACH MONTH
BECAUSE HE IS STILL EMPLOYED. HE IS A PHOTOCOPIER FOR I-B-M AND
MAKES 20-THOUSAND DOLLARS A YEAR. UNDER THE LAW, SMITH IS
ENTITLED TO THE SOCIAL SECURITY CHECKS LIKE ANY OTHER CITIZEN
HIS AGE, PROVIDED HE MAKES NO MORE THAN THREE-THOUSAND
DOLLARS A YEAR. THE SMITHS HAVE MADE REPEATED CALLS TO THE
SOCIAL SECURITY ADMINISTRATION IN AN EFFORT TO GET THE CHECKS
STOPPED. THEY ARE WORRIED THAT WHEN ORVAL DOES RETIRE, HE
MIGHT HAVE TROUBLE COLLECTING THE MONEY THAT WILL BE DUE
HIM. THE SMITHS BELIEVE THE GOVERNMENT CONTINUES TO SEND THE
CHECKS BECAUSE OF A COMPUTER MALFUNCTION. ORVAL SMITH
APPLIED FOR MEDICARE, WHICH HE DID NOT WANT BUT WAS
ENTITLED TO, ON HIS SIXTY-FIFTH BIRTHDAY. THAT WAS A MISTAKE,
SAYS SMITH. EVIDENTLY THE COMPUTER ALSO ENROLLED HIM IN
SOCIAL SECURITY RETIREMENT BENEFITS.

Example 2

STEP 1—INITIAL STATEMENT, THE LEAD:
BLACK NATIONALIST GUERRILLAS ARE SUSPECTED OF CAUSING THE
CRASH OF A RHODESIAN AIRLINER.

STEP 2—REPEATS THE LEAD STATEMENT IN DIFFERENT WORDS:
AIRE RHODESIA OFFICIALS BELIEVE THE GROUP IS RESPONSIBLE FOR
SHOOTING THE PLANE DOWN SHORTLY AFTER IT TOOK OFF FROM
KARIBA.

STEP 3—GIVES DETAILS OR EXAMPLES TO ILLUSTRATE STEP 1:
THE PLANE MADE A DISTRESS CALL SIX MINUTES AFTER IT TOOK OFF
AND THEN CRASHED.

STEP 4—ASSIGNS THE ORIGIN OR CAUSE OF STEP 1 STATEMENT:
GUERRILLAS CLAIM RESPONSIBILITY FOR DOWNING A RHODESIAN
PLANE IN A SIMILAR MANNER LAST SEPTEMBER.

STEP 5—COMPARES SIMILAR IDEAS OR PHENOMENA WITH STEP 1:
BOTH PLANES WERE FOUR-ENGINE TURBOPROP VISCOUNTS DEPARTING
FROM KARIBA.

STEP 6—CONTRASTS DISSIMILAR IDEAS OR PHENOMENA WITH STEP 1:
HOWEVER, AUTHORITIES DO NOT HAVE ENOUGH EVIDENCE TO LINK
THE SEPTEMBER CRASH TO THIS RECENT INCIDENT.

STEP 7—STATES OR PROGNOSTICATES THE RESULTS OR CONCLUSION:
ALL 59 PASSENGERS AND CREW MEMBERS WERE KILLED.

Here is the story without the steps indicated.

BLACK NATIONALIST GUERRILLAS ARE SUSPECTED OF CAUSING THE
CRASH OF A RHODESIAN AIRLINER. AIRE RHODESIA OFFICIALS
BELIEVE THE GROUP IS RESPONSIBLE FOR SHOOTING THE PLANE DOWN
SHORTLY AFTER IT TOOK OFF FROM KARIBA. THE PLANE MADE A
DISTRESS CALL SIX MINUTES AFTER IT TOOK OFF AND THEN CRASHED.
GUERRILLAS CLAIM RESPONSIBILITY FOR DOWNING A RHODESIAN
PLANE IN A SIMILAR MANNER LAST SEPTEMBER. BOTH PLANES WERE
FOUR-ENGINE TURBOPROP VISCOUNTS DEPARTING FROM KARIBA.
HOWEVER, THE AUTHORITIES DO NOT HAVE ENOUGH EVIDENCE TO
LINK THE SEPTEMBER CRASH TO THIS RECENT INCIDENT. ALL 59
PASSENGERS AND CREW MEMBERS WERE KILLED.

ASSIGNMENTS: WRITING THE SEVEN-STEP NEWS STORY

1. Use a newspaper or a newspaper wire service as a news source.
2. Select and clip a story from these sources for each of the following

types of stories: local, state, regional, national, international. Mount each clipping on an 8½-×-11-inch sheet of typing paper. Be sure the sheet is identified with your name, class, date, and the nature of the assignment. Your instructor may wish additional identification.

3. From each clipping work out a detailed fact sheet. You will write your story from this fact sheet. Think of it as being the equivalent of a fact sheet that you have prepared as a reporter on the job. Be sure to avoid using the original writer's phrases and descriptions.

4. Select fact sheets from the five types of stories and write as many of the following leads—hard news, soft news, literary allusion or parody lead, question lead—as your instructor assigns.

5. Study the fact sheets you have prepared. If the leads you have written are adequate, use them. If not, rewrite or write new ones.

6. Be sure to identify each step as you begin writing your story one step at a time. Use the identification procedure found in the explanatory illustrations. For example, Step 1—Initial Statement. Follow this with your lead. Then go on to Steps 2, 3, and so on. Following this step-by-step routine will help you develop an intuitive feeling about writing.

7. Finally, type a double-spaced copy of each news story you have written on a separate page. This routine gives you a chance to review and revise your story by checking and rechecking. Repetitious discipline is the quickest way to develop intuitive action. That is why all writing routines should be carried out as efficiently as possible until they become habitual (like typing). This is also the procedure one employs in making a cake from a recipe. If repeated regularly and often enough your procedure becomes so habitual that you work intuitively. In the same way your ability to write becomes intuitive.

8. When you turn in an assignment, remember that your instructor may want the following: a copy of your source; a copy of your fact sheet; a step-by-step copy of your written news story; a copy of your story prepared without the steps. Naturally each copy should be adequately identified.

Modifying the Seven-step Newswriting Process, Omitting One or More Steps

On occasion, if your story needs to be shortened to fit a specific time slot, one or more of the seven steps may be omitted. In general, all the steps may be left out except 1 and 7. On occasion one or more of Steps 2, 3, 4, 5, or 6 may be needed to clarify details and/or add interest to a story. Also keep in mind that the steps after 1 and 2 need not be in the order given here, with one exception. Step 7 is last.

The luxury car news story would be as follows if Steps 3, 4, 5, and 6 were omitted.

STEP 1—INITIAL STATEMENT, THE LEAD:
THE LARGE AMERICAN CAR IS LOSING ITS STATUS AS A SYMBOL OF
LUXURY.

STEP 2—REPEATS THE LEAD CONCEPT IN DIFFERENT WORDS:
REPORTS SHOW THAT MOST BUYERS ARE LEAVING THEM IN THE
SHOWROOM.

STEP 7—STATES OR PROGNOSTICATES THE RESULTS OR CONCLUSION:
AS ONE DRIVER PUT IT, THE SYMBOL OF LUXURY IN AUTOMOBILES
TODAY BELONGS TO THE CAR THAT COSTS LESS AND SAVES GAS, NOT
USES IT.

Here is how the story looks without the steps indicated.

THE LARGE AMERICAN CAR IS LOSING ITS STATUS AS A SYMBOL OF
LUXURY. REPORTS SHOW THAT MOST BUYERS ARE LEAVING THEM IN
THE SHOWROOM. AS ONE DRIVER PUT IT, THE SYMBOL OF LUXURY IN
AUTOMOBILES TODAY BELONGS TO THE CAR THAT COSTS LESS AND
SAVES GAS, NOT USES IT.

One way of determining what may be left out of a seven-step news
story when it needs shortening is to omit different steps as you read it. The
story, while not as complete, must make sense without the omitted
portions. The same concept also applies when writing a modified seven-
step news story from a fact sheet. And radio writing requires shorter
stories. On occasion a story will not have enough facts to permit you to
develop it in detail.

Analyzing the Modified Seven-step Process News Story

A practical way to develop an intuitive feeling about modifying a seven-
step news story is to analyze copy. Look at each of the following stories
and determine which step or steps of the Seven-step Process were omitted.
Also identify the steps that were retained.

Example 1

FRENCH SCIENTISTS ANNOUNCED THE PERFECTION OF A NEW CANCER
DRUG. SHOULD THE FRENCH DISCOVERY PROVE EFFECTIVE AS
EXPECTED, THOUSANDS OF LIVES MAY BE SAVED. FRENCH OFFICIALS
ARE URGING MEDICAL AUTHORITIES AROUND THE WORLD TO TEST
THE NEW DRUG.

Example 2

THE IRISH REPUBLIC'S PRIME MINISTER, 63-YEAR-OLD JACK RIGGS, IS
GETTING READY TO RESIGN. HE ASKED THE PARLIAMENTARY
MEMBERS OF THE GOVERNING PARTY TO CHOOSE A SUCCESSOR AS
SOON AS POSSIBLE. RIGGS IS BEING CRITICIZED FOR HIS DOMESTIC
POLICIES AND HIS RELATIVELY MODERATE APPROACH TO THE
PROBLEM OF NORTHERN IRELAND. RIGGS SAYS HE IS BEING
PRESSURED TO QUIT.

Example 3

ON WALL STREET TODAY, THE DOW JONES CLOSING WAS UP A LITTLE
OVER FIVE-AND-A-QUARTER POINTS AT EIGHT-TWENTY-FOUR-POINT-
NINE. THE AVERAGE PRICE PER SHARE WAS 27-CENTS, WITH TODAY'S
VOLUME 33-AND-ONE-HALF-MILLION SHARES. ON THE AMERICAN
EXCHANGE, THE VOLUME WAS FOUR-MILLION-23-THOUSAND SHARES.
THE AVERAGE PRICE IS UP 12-CENTS.

Example 4

THE DEPARTMENT OF HEALTH, EDUCATION, AND WELFARE TODAY
ANNOUNCED NEW GUIDELINES FOR ENDING SEX BIAS IN COLLEGE
ATHLETICS AT SCHOOLS THAT RECEIVE FEDERAL AID. H-E-W
SECRETARY PATRICIA HARRIS SAID THE NEW RULES INCLUDED A
DECREE ON SPORTS SCHOLARSHIPS. FULL DETAILS ARE BEING SENT TO
ALL COLLEGES AND UNIVERSITIES. AUTHORITIES AT THE LOCAL
UNIVERSITY WERE NOT AVAILABLE FOR COMMENT.

Writing the Modified Seven-step News Story

The short version of the Seven-step Process is useful for writing brief news
messages. Suppose, for example, you have collected information about a
hurricane that is headed toward the city where you work as a broadcast
newswriter. In fact, your station is the prime source for the news going
out about it. That means you are in constant touch with all available authorities. You have already written several updates on the progress of the
storm. Now it is time to give the listener-viewer the latest hard news information about it.

As you write Step 1, the lead, for your brief story, you know that it
must furnish an answer to what is happening and where the hurricane is

located. These are important questions in the listener-viewer's mind. You shouldn't have any trouble getting his or her attention, but you take no chances.

STEP 1—INITIAL STATEMENT, THE LEAD:
HERE IS THE LATEST REPORT ON HURRICANE IVEY.

This statement is designed to get attention and tell the listener-viewer what the central idea of your message will be.

Next you need to provide facts about the hurricane. The facts for your statement are from the Weather Bureau. Therefore you must state what the hurricane is doing and where it is headed. You will also link what you write about the hurricane to the listener-viewer's life and the inevitable concern each has for the safety of family, property, and friends. This means you will need to use Step 3 of the Seven-step Process because with it you can give essential details.

STEP 3—GIVES DETAILS OR EXAMPLES TO ILLUSTRATE STEP 1:
THE STORM IS NOW MOVING TOWARD LAND AT THE RATE OF 13-MILES AN HOUR. THE WEATHER BUREAU SAYS THAT IF THE 100-MILE-AN-HOUR HURRICANE CONTINUES ON ITS PRESENT COURSE. IT WILL BE CENTERED OVER THE CITY BY TOMORROW NIGHT.

Such a statement brings the hurricane and the listener-viewer closer together. You've answered the most important of all questions about it. You've told him or her when the storm may arrive. In this way you let the listener-viewer know how the storm may affect the lives of those in the city and the area surrounding it.

Next your message must let the listener-viewer know the answer to additional questions about the storm. You have implied how bad it is—100 miles an hour—but what should the listener-viewer do to prepare for it? Your responsibility is to give the listener-viewer an answer. You do this by adding authority to your facts. You must tell the listener-viewer just who is making the objective judgment about what each of them should do.

Because you want to keep the message as short as possible you turn to the last step in the Seven-step Process.

STEP 7—STATES OR PROGNOSTICATES THE RESULTS OR CONCLUSION:
THE WEATHER BUREAU SAYS THAT ALL KNOWN PRECAUTIONARY MEASURES SHOULD BE TAKEN IMMEDIATELY. LAW OFFICIALS SAY THAT ALL PEOPLE LIVING IN LOW AREAS OR NEAR THE COAST SHOULD PACK ADEQUATE PERSONAL BELONGINGS AND MOVE TO PUBLIC SHELTER IMMEDIATELY. STAY TUNED FOR FURTHER DETAILS.

Those three steps of the Seven-step Process include all the information that is needed at this time about the hurricane. Your entire story is factual, specific, and authoritative. It is, therefore, believable and is a message your listener-viewer can trust. Here is the story in its entirety.

> HERE IS THE LATEST REPORT ON HURRICANE IVEY. THE STORM IS NOW MOVING TOWARD LAND AT THE RATE OF 13-MILES AN HOUR. THE WEATHER BUREAU SAYS THAT IF THE 100-MILE-AN-HOUR HURRICANE CONTINUES ON ITS PRESENT COURSE, IT WILL BE CENTERED OVER THE CITY BY TOMORROW NIGHT. THE WEATHER BUREAU SAYS THAT ALL KNOWN PRECAUTIONARY MEASURES SHOULD BE TAKEN IMMEDIATELY. LAW OFFICIALS SAY THAT ALL PEOPLE LIVING IN LOW AREAS OR NEAR THE COAST SHOULD PACK ADEQUATE PERSONAL BELONGINGS AND MOVE TO PUBLIC SHELTERS IMMEDIATELY. STAY TUNED FOR FURTHER DETAILS.

ASSIGNMENTS: WRITING THE MODIFIED SEVEN-STEP PROCESS

Select data and prepare fact sheets. This time, however, write modified seven-step news stories. Let the need for certain facts determine the steps used or omitted. Make each story as short and as succinct as possible. Use the following kinds of leads for each story: hard news lead and soft news lead.

Write as many of each as time permits and your need as a writer dictates. As usual turn in: a copy of your source material; a copy of your fact sheet; a step-by-step copy of your written news story; a copy of your story without the steps indicated.

NEWSWRITING AND VIDEOTAPE

Most of the news that is used to illustrate this chapter, as well as the stories you have written for the Six-step Process assignments, were for anchor persons or radio newscasters. Once you become adept at writing these stories it is relatively easy to coordinate what you write with videotape or film.

As you know, the purpose of any visual is to illustrate. The use of videotape approximates the expression "Seeing is believing." Rarely, however, is videotape used to the exclusion of all verbal explanation. Therefore, the question is, "How much of each TV news story should be seen and how much should be heard?"

Learning how to coordinate the verbal with the visual is gained by experience. It is therefore best acquired after you are on the job and can work with a professional and with adequate equipment. However, there are a few basic considerations about blending words with pictures that you should take with you.

For example, many writers tend to *hear* a news story being spoken as they write. They are likely to tell you that videotape is secondary and should be used only to illustrate what is said. Those who are visual-minded, however, tend to see a news story as action. They are likely to say, "One picture is worth a thousand words."

Most news professionals who spend their lives turning H-O-E-Os into stories for listener-viewers eventually discover that deciding how much should be words and how much should be videotape is a relative matter. For example, sometimes what is written is based entirely on a preview of the videotape previously shot at an H-O-E-O scene. Sometimes the news story you are to write will require a continuous visual presentation. What is written on such an occasion may be heard but it is background and the reporter is never seen. On other occasions you will be asked to write your script and turn it over to the videotape editor, who will supply the visuals he believes are needed. Another procedure requires the writer to prepare a card for the video editor. This card lists the general type of video shots wanted and the time-length of each story segment. The verbal and the video may then be coordinated by a third person. Sometimes the writer has a special camera crew and directs the video and writes the entire story.

These methods, plus many variations, are used by most television stations. The procedure preferred by a station depends on the budget, the equipment available, the size and experience of the news staff, and the preference that has previously been established.

The following story reports the activity at a senior citizen center. Study the Seven-step Process analysis of the story and then turn to the broadcast script.

Example

STEP 1—INITIAL STATEMENT, THE LEAD:
THE SENIOR CITIZENS CENTER, LOCATED AT FIRST AND HUBBARD, OFFERS A VARIETY OF SERVICES FOR SENIORS . . . EVERYTHING FROM HEALTH ADVICE, EDUCATION, CLUB MEETINGS, TO A NUTRITIOUS MEAL.

STEP 2—REPEATS THE LEAD STATEMENT IN DIFFERENT WORDS:
WHATEVER THE NEED, THE CENTER TRIES TO PROVIDE IT THROUGH SCHEDULED ACTIVITIES.

STEP 3—GIVES DETAILS OR EXAMPLES TO ILLUSTRATE STEP 1:
AND WHAT IS THE RESPONSE FROM SENIORS? [SOUND ON TAPE:
BARBARA BROOKS: "OVERWHELMING . . . FROM THE FIRST DAY
ACTIVITIES WELL SUPPORTED . . . PLEASED WITH RESPONSE FROM
SENIORS."]

STEP 4—ASSIGNS THE ORIGIN OR CAUSE OF STEP 1 STATEMENT:
[SENIORS ON VIDEO] THE LARGEST ACTIVITY AT THE CENTER IS THE
NUTRITION PROGRAM WHICH SERVES ABOUT 200 A DAY. IN ADDITION,
THE SENIORS ALSO LEARN NUTRITION EDUCATION. A NEW PROGRAM
THAT HAS BEEN WELL ACCEPTED FOCUSES ON PHYSICAL FITNESS AND
OFFERS DAILY EXERCISE CLASSES AND ACTIVITY.

STEP 5—COMPARES SIMILAR IDEAS OR PHENOMENA WITH STEP 1:
THE CENTER, OPEN MONDAY THROUGH FRIDAY WITH CERTAIN
SCHEDULED EVENTS ON THE WEEKEND, HAS A PAID STAFF.

STEP 6—CONTRASTS DISSIMILAR IDEAS OR PHENOMENA WITH STEP 1:
BUT ACCORDING TO BROOKS, THE CENTER COULD NOT RUN ALL OF ITS
ACTIVITIES WITHOUT THE HELP OF ITS VOLUNTEERS.

STEP 7—STATES OR PROGNOSTICATES THE RESULTS OR CONCLUSION:
[TAG IN FRONT OF CENTER:] THE SENIOR CITIZENS CENTER IS A
CENTRAL PLACE FOR SENIORS TO COME TOGETHER AND GET
INVOLVED IN MANY PROGRAMS AND ACTIVITIES. CINDY JONES,
TELEVISION 12, ACTION NEWS.

Now the story as it was turned in to the News Director:

SR. CITIZEN CENTER   SOT 1:15

    SLUG

C. JONES

Writer

(Seniors video):   THE SENIOR CITIZENS CENTER,
                                LOCATED AT FIRST AND HUBBARD,
                                OFFERS A VARIETY OF SERVICES FOR
                                SENIORS . . . EVERYTHING FROM
                                HEALTH ADVICE, EDUCATION, CLUB
                                MEETINGS, TO A NUTRITIOUS MEAL.
                                WHATEVER IS NEEDED, THE CENTER

	TRYS TO PROVIDE IT THROUGH SCHEDULED ACTIVITIES. AND WHAT IS THE RESPONSE FROM SENIORS?
SOT: Barbara Brooks:	"OVERWHELMING . . . FROM THE FIRST DAY ACTIVITIES WELL SUPPORTED . . . PLEASED WITH RESPONSE FROM SENIORS."
(Seniors video):	THE LARGEST ACTIVITY AT THE CENTER IS THE NUTRITION PROGRAM WHICH SERVES ABOUT 200 A DAY. IN ADDITION, THE SENIORS ALSO LEARN NUTRITION EDUCATION. A NEW PROGRAM THAT HAS BEEN WELL ACCEPTED FOCUSES ON PHYSICAL FITNESS AND OFFERS DAILY EXERCISE CLASSES AND ACTIVITY.
	THE CENTER, OPEN MONDAY THROUGH FRIDAY WITH CERTAIN SCHEDULED EVENTS ON THE WEEKEND, HAS A PAID STAFF. BUT ACCORDING TO BROOKS, THE CENTER COULD NOT RUN ALL OF ITS ACTIVITIES WITHOUT THE HELP OF ITS VOLUNTEERS.
Stand-up TAG in front of center:	THE SENIOR CITIZENS CENTER OFFERS A MULTITUDE OF SERVICES AND IS A CENTRAL PLACE FOR SENIORS TO COME TOGETHER AND GET INVOLVED IN MANY PROGRAMS AND ACTIVITIES. CINDY JONES, TELEVISION 12, ACTION NEWS.

ADDING SUSPENSE TO A NEWS STORY: THE FIVE–STEP PROCESS

All news stories, whether for radio or television, can be made more interesting, more dramatic, by using the basic principle of suspense called *conflict*. Conflict consists of opposing actions, incompatibilities, divergent ideas, human interests, personal drives, wishes, internal or external demands. When conflict is present in an H-O-E-O, it produces a circumstance or situation that must be settled or resolved, even when there seems to be no way of doing so.

The time-honored way of introducing suspense into a news story is with the Five-step Process. You learn to use it in much the same way that you learned to use the Six-step and the Seven-step Processes.

First, the writer must understand the Five-step's organizational development. Here are the details for that purpose. As usual Step 1 is the lead.

Step 1. Situation and Characterization Statement—Lead In the lead, you the writer introduce the person(s) and the situation(s) that involves the person(s) in a conflict. Your character(s) and the situation(s) should be of such a nature, or so stated by you, that the listener-viewer's attention is caught immediately. Conflict is created by bringing the character(s) face to face with a problem about which there is considerable feeling, but over which, at that particular time, the character(s) has little control. Nonetheless, the problem must be solved, and in an effort to resolve it, additional conflicts are created.

Step 2. Rising Action Additional complications, conflicts consisting of action and reaction, should be introduced so that the listener-viewer's interest is heightened by wondering, even before the potential solution is suggested, just what the result will be. The element that creates this interest is called *suspense*. Such complications are essential because conflict and complication are the essence of every exciting news story, just as they are the essence of every involvement in life. Therefore you should develop as many complications as possible from the fact sheet and use them, or imply their presence, in Step 2.

Keep in mind, however, that the complication(s) always arises or grows out of the effort(s) being exerted to solve the preceding complication. And there is always some question as to whether the character(s) can or will solve it.

Step 3. Climax The climax is that point of action and development in your story at which the problem, with its conflict(s), reaches its highest point of action and is resolved, not settled. (The hero merely overcomes the villain.) It is during this point in your story that an action occurs or is taken (the tide is turned) for or against your character(s). The climax is the turning point in the story.

Step 4. Falling Action Because every turning point must be explained, Step 4 is referred to as the period of falling action. It is that period in your story, following the climax, during which there is action that resolves the conflict(s) that existed before the climax. This period of falling action takes your character(s) through the essential actions, reactions, or responses that explain the effect of the climax on the situation(s).

Step 5. Denouement or Outcome The denouement or outcome explains how the events or considerations after the climax are finally settled for or against your character(s). The denouement or outcome is an explanation of what finally happens to your character(s) and gives the character(s)'s final action or reaction to having been through the various conflicts and situations. Obviously the denouement or outcome is the end of your news story.

How to Use the Five-step Process

Before you begin writing a Five-step Process news story, be sure to find and develop all the conflicting events and actions you can find in your H-O-E-O. Be sure your information has those human aspects called conflict. Conflict catches and holds listener-viewer attention. In addition to using conflict, be sure to use the technique of comparison, not just superlatives, to help develop a feeling of excitement. For example, use such phrases as:

- THE BIGGEST TAX CUT SINCE . . .
- THE LARGEST BUDGET DEFICIT . . .
- THE WORST HURRICANE OF THIS SEASON . . .
- THE FIRST FOOTBALL PLAYER TO WALK OFF THE FIELD SINCE . . .

Each comparison stimulates the imagination because it implies conflict. Remember that every conflict you develop, or imply, will give your story additional dramatic action. This is especially true when each succeeding conflict grows out of the preceding conflict. It is this kind of dramatic action that makes a news story more interesting.

Study the following news stories. They illustrate how the Five-step Process may be used to develop suspense.

The first example is a situation that illustrates how the mechanics of the Five-step Process may be used by an imaginative writer to give excitement and life to an otherwise mundane H-O-E-O. Here is the fact sheet.

1. There has been a wreck. A car was hit in the side by an 18-wheeler.
2. Harry Davis, father, 42, and his son, John, 20, were in the car.
3. The father and son forgot about a stoplight and drove into the intersection of the truck route that travels around Centerville.

4. The two men were on their way to work, driving on Highway 90, which crosses the truck route.

5. The father said he was "giving his son fits" at the time of the accident for staying out late at night and for not going to church on Sunday.

6. The Davis car was totaled by the 18-wheeler and carried 400 feet along the highway before falling into a ditch.

7. Both men were bruised but neither was seriously hurt. Harry Davis said they were saved by the Almighty.

8. John Davis, the son, said he would give some close thought to his father's suggestions about going to church.

9. The truck suffered minor damage. Its driver, Harold Houston, continued his trip within an hour.

10. Davis was charged with running a red light.

Ordinarily an accident of this nature is ignored as news, unless similar ones have occurred at the same place. But as a young ambitious reporter, you decide to do a feature. You look over your notes, the fact sheet, and because there is a possible human interest angle, you begin thinking in terms of the Five-step Process. First you need a lead around which to build the story, so you begin by stating the obvious.

Example 1

STEP 1—SITUATION AND CHARACTER—LEAD:
FROM CENTERVILLE THIS MORNING COMES THE STORY OF TWO MEN,
HARRY DAVIS AND HIS 20-YEAR-OLD-SON, JOHN. THE TWO MEN,
DRIVING ALONG STATE HIGHWAY 90, WERE ON THEIR WAY TO WORK.
THEY WERE ALSO ENGAGED IN A HEATED FATHER-SON DISCUSSION.

That lead establishes the fact that two men in a car are driving to work on Highway 90 and are arguing about something, which in turn implies that in all probability they weren't watching what they were doing or where they were going. Their arguing is conflict, and not watching what they are doing is a form of conflict.

Next in your story, after establishing the situation and the characters, you need additional conflict, if possible, to give your story more suspense. You look over your fact sheet and decide to describe what happened to them.

STEP 2—RISING ACTION:
NEITHER OF THE DAVISES WAS AWARE THEY WERE ENTERING A
TRUCK ROUTE CROSSING. AS THEIR CAR MOVED INTO THE

INTERSECTION, THEY SAW A LOADED 18-WHEELER ROARING TOWARD
THEM. STUNNED BY THE TRUCK'S SUDDEN APPEARANCE, THE TWO
MEN CRINGED IN THE FRONT SEAT. THE TRUCK DRIVER, SEEING THE
CAR, SLAMMED ON HIS BRAKES.

You have developed a good deal of suspense. Now your listener-
viewer will want to know what happened to the car, the truck, and the
occupants. You look over your fact sheet and write the climax.

STEP 3—CLIMAX:
RUBBER SMOKE BOILED UP FROM THE SCREECHING TRUCK TIRES AS
THE 18-WHEELER PLOWED INTO THE CAR, FLATTENING IT AGAINST
THE TRUCK'S FRONT END AND BUMPER. THE CRUMPLED CAR WAS
CARRIED 400-FEET ALONG THE TRUCK ROUTE AND TOSSED INTO A
DITCH.

Now you've written the climax, the peak of your story, without
revealing the outcome. That is as it should be. This means that the next
thing your listener-viewer will want to know is were the two men badly
hurt, or were they perhaps killed? You look over your fact sheet and write:

STEP 4—FALLING ACTION:
BUT BEFORE THE TRUCK DRIVER COULD BRING HIS RIG TO A
COMPLETE STOP, DAVIS AND HIS SON CRAWLED OUT OF THEIR
BATTERED AND BUCKLED WRECK. THEY WERE SHAKEN AND
SCRATCHED, BUT UNHURT.

This unit of falling action lets the listener-viewer know how the
characters made it through the climactic action. Now you need to complete
the story, using other information from your fact sheet. The next step, the
denouement or outcome, brings the story to a close.

STEP 5—DENOUEMENT OR OUTCOME:
WHEN THE HIGHWAY PATROL ARRIVED, THE ELDER DAVIS RECEIVED
A TICKET FOR RUNNING A RED LIGHT. HE SAID GETTING IT WAS ALL
RIGHT BECAUSE HE'D JUST FINISHED TELLING HIS SON HE SHOULD
STOP DRINKING AND STAYING OUT AT NIGHT, AND GO TO CHURCH. HE
SAID THEY WERE SAVED BY THE ALMIGHTY. WHEN ASKED HIS VIEWS,
SON JOHN SAID IT WAS A CLOSE CALL, AND HE WAS DEFINITELY GOING
TO GIVE HIS DAD'S SUGGESTION SOME THOUGHT.

Review the content of each step and note how each one is put
together. Analyze each carefully and determine which steps in the Five-
step Process are constructed after the pattern of the Six-step or the Seven-

step Processes. Always think in terms of these two processes to help you until your writing technique becomes intuitive.

Here is the story in detail:

FROM CENTERVILLE THIS MORNING COMES THE STORY OF TWO MEN, HARRY DAVIS AND HIS 20-YEAR-OLD SON, JOHN. THE TWO MEN, DRIVING ALONG STATE HIGHWAY 90, WERE ON THEIR WAY TO WORK. THEY WERE ALSO ENGAGED IN A HEATED FATHER-SON DISCUSSION.

NEITHER OF THE DAVISES WAS AWARE THEY WERE ENTERING A TRUCK ROUTE CROSSING. AS THEIR CAR MOVED INTO THE INTERSECTION, THEY SAW A LOADED 18-WHEELER ROARING TOWARD THEM. STUNNED BY THE TRUCK'S SUDDEN APPEARANCE THE TWO MEN CRINGED IN THE FRONT SEAT. THE TRUCK DRIVER, SEEING THE CAR, SLAMMED ON HIS BRAKES.

RUBBER SMOKE BOILED UP FROM THE SCREECHING TRUCK TIRES AS THE 18-WHEELER PLOWED INTO THE CAR, FLATTENING IT AGAINST THE TRUCK'S FRONT END AND BUMPER. THE CRUMPLED CAR WAS CARRIED 400-FEET ALONG THE TRUCK ROUTE AND TOSSED INTO A DITCH. BUT BEFORE THE TRUCK DRIVER COULD BRING HIS RIG TO A COMPLETE STOP, DAVIS AND HIS SON CRAWLED OUT OF THEIR BATTERED AND BUCKLED WRECK. THEY WERE SHAKEN AND SCRATCHED, BUT UNHURT.

WHEN THE HIGHWAY PATROL ARRIVED, THE ELDER DAVIS RECEIVED A TICKET FOR RUNNING A RED LIGHT. HE SAID GETTING IT WAS ALL RIGHT BECAUSE HE'D JUST FINISHED TELLING HIS SON HE SHOULD STOP DRINKING AND STAYING OUT AT NIGHT, AND GO TO CHURCH. HE SAID THEY WERE SAVED BY THE ALMIGHTY. WHEN ASKED HIS VIEWS, SON JOHN SAID IT WAS A CLOSE CALL, AND HE WAS DEFINITELY GOING TO GIVE HIS DAD'S SUGGESTION SOME THOUGHT.

The Five-step Process Sports Story

The following Five-step Process story illustrates how a writer may put more excitement in a sports story. As you read it be sure to refer to the definitions for each step. Doing so will help you discover how best to incorporate the Five-step Process into your writing technique. Also think of how you may use the various steps from the Six- and Seven-step Processes to help you develop details in each step of the Five-step Process.

Example 1

STEP 1—SITUATION AND CHARACTER—LEAD:
IN TATUM GYM LAST NIGHT, THE UNIVERSITY BEARCATS TOOK ON 13TH-RANKED EASTERN KENTUCKY.

STEP 2—RISING ACTION:

HALFWAY THROUGH THE FIRST PERIOD, THE "CATS" WERE AHEAD 19-TO-8 WHEN BOTH LAWRENCE GRAY AND GREG JONES FOULED OUT.

STEP 3—CLIMAX:

BUT WITH AN UPSURGE OF TALENT THE BEARCATS HELD ON TO A CLOSE LEAD UNTIL ZACK DAVIS, STARTING IN THE SECOND HALF, RESPONDED BY HELPING THE "CATS" HANG UP A 93-TO-60 VICTORY.

STEP 4—FALLING ACTION:

THE FINAL 33-POINT MARGIN WAS THE LARGEST OF THE NIGHT. THE BEARCATS OUT-SCORED THE EASTERN KENTUCKIANS BY 23-TO-5 IN THE LAST FOUR MINUTES.

STEP 5—DENOUEMENT OR OUTCOME:

COACH DANLEY SAID AFTER THE GAME THAT THE TEAM DEVELOPED A WINNING FORM. THE VICTORY OVER THE EASTERN KENTUCKIANS PUTS THE "CATS" AT FOUR WINS AND ONE LOSS FOR THE SEASON.

Here is the story without the steps indicated.

IN TATUM GYM LAST NIGHT THE UNIVERSITY BEARCATS TOOK ON 13TH–RANKED EASTERN KENTUCKY. HALFWAY THROUGH THE FIRST PERIOD, THE "CATS" WERE AHEAD 19-TO-8 WHEN BOTH LAWRENCE GRAY AND GREG JONES FOULED OUT. BUT WITH AN UPSURGE OF TALENT THE BEARCATS HELD ON TO A CLOSE LEAD UNTIL ZACK DAVIS, STARTING IN THE SECOND HALF, RESPONDED BY HELPING THE "CATS" HANG UP A 93-TO-60 VICTORY. THE FINAL 33-POINT MARGIN WAS THE LARGEST OF THE NIGHT. THE BEARCATS OUT-SCORED THE EASTERN KENTUCKIANS BY 23-TO-5 IN THE LAST FOUR MINUTES. COACH DANLEY SAID AFTER THE GAME THAT THE TEAM DEVELOPED A WINNING FORM. THE VICTORY OVER THE EASTERN KENTUCKIANS PUTS THE "CATS" AT FOUR WINS AND ONE LOSS FOR THE SEASON.

Example 2

STEP 1—SITUATION AND CHARACTER:

YESTERDAY IN THE QUARTER FINALS MATCH OF THE FRENCH OPEN TENNIS CLASSIC IN PARIS, BJORN BORG TOOK ON SOUTH AFRICAN TENNIS SENSATION RAY MOORE.

STEP 2—RISING ACTION:

BORG, PLAYING WITH AN INJURED RIGHT THUMB, WORRIED HIS FANS BY LOSING THE FIRST TWO GAMES OF THE MATCH.

STEP 3—CLIMAX:
DURING THE THIRD GAME, HOWEVER, BORG BEGAN PLAYING LIKE
THE WORLD CHAMPION THAT HE IS. IN AN AMAZING DISPLAY OF
TENNIS SKILL, BORG DEFEATED MOORE SIX-THREE, SIX-ONE, SIX-LOVE.

STEP 4—FALLING ACTION:
THE SCORE'S MARGIN IS THE LARGEST TURNED IN SO FAR AT THE
TOURNAMENT.

STEP 5—DENOUEMENT OR OUTCOME:
IF SUCCESSFUL AGAINST ROSCOE TANNER IN HIS SEMIFINAL MATCH,
BORG WILL ONCE AGAIN TAKE ON JIMMY CONNORS FOR THE
CHAMPIONSHIP.

Here is the story without the steps indicated.

YESTERDAY IN THE QUARTER FINALS MATCH OF THE FRENCH OPEN
TENNIS CLASSIC IN PARIS, BJORN BORG ONCE AGAIN TOOK ON SOUTH
AFRICAN TENNIS SENSATION RAY MOORE. BORG, PLAYING WITH AN
INJURED RIGHT THUMB, WORRIED HIS FANS BY LOSING THE FIRST TWO
GAMES OF THE MATCH. DURING THE THIRD GAME, HOWEVER, BORG
BEGAN PLAYING LIKE THE WORLD CHAMPION HE IS. IN AN AMAZING
DISPLAY OF TENNIS SKILL, BORG DEFEATED MOORE SIX-THREE,
SIX-ONE, SIX-LOVE. THE SCORE'S MARGIN IS THE LARGEST TURNED IN SO
FAR AT THE TOURNAMENT. IF SUCCESSFUL AGAINST ROSCOE TANNER
IN HIS SEMIFINALS MATCH, BORG WILL ONCE AGAIN TAKE ON JIMMY
CONNORS FOR THE CHAMPIONSHIP.

The Five-step Process Human Interest Story

Example 1

STEP 1—SITUATION AND CHARACTER—LEAD:
THE POSTAL SERVICE SLOGAN COVERS RAIN, SLEET, SNOW, AND
GLOOM OF NIGHT, BUT MAILMAN FRANCIS EMERSON MAY BE
THINKING IT SHOULD SAY SOMETHING ABOUT CERTAIN KINDS OF
BITES.

STEP 2—RISING ACTION:
EMERSON WAS DELIVERING A WELFARE CHECK TO 24-YEAR-OLD
GLADYS ROACH OF 611 WEST 37TH-STREET. MRS. ROACH TOLD HIM TO
HAND HER THE CHECK, BUT EMERSON EXPLAINED THAT POSTAL

REGULATIONS REQUIRE HE PLACE THE ENVELOPE WITH HER CHECK IN THE BOX.

STEP 3—CLIMAX:
EMERSON REACHED TO PUT THE ENVELOPE IN THE BOX, AND MRS. ROACH ALLEGEDLY GRABBED HIS RIGHT HAND AND SANK HER TEETH INTO IT.

STEP 4—FALLING ACTION:
IN FELONY COURT TODAY, MRS. ROACH'S ATTORNEY ARGUED THAT HIS CLIENT'S TEETH WERE FALSE AND COULDN'T HAVE DONE MUCH DAMAGE.

STEP 5—DENOUEMENT OR OUTCOME:
MAGISTRATE NATHAN BUTTERFIELD DIDN'T SEE IT THAT WAY. HE SET BAIL AT 500-DOLLARS AND ORDERED MRS. ROACH TO STAND TRIAL ON CHARGES OF ASSAULT.

Here is the story without the steps indicated.

THE POSTAL SERVICE SLOGAN COVERS RAIN, SLEET, SNOW, AND GLOOM OF NIGHT, BUT MAILMAN FRANCIS EMERSON MAY BE THINKING IT SHOULD SAY SOMETHING ABOUT CERTAIN KINDS OF BITES. EMERSON WAS DELIVERING A WELFARE CHECK TO 24-YEAR-OLD GLADYS ROACH OF 611 WEST 37TH-STREET. MRS. ROACH TOLD HIM TO HAND HER THE CHECK, BUT EMERSON EXPLAINED THAT POSTAL REGULATIONS REQUIRE HE PLACE THE ENVELOPE WITH THE CHECK IN THE BOX. EMERSON REACHED TO PUT THE ENVELOPE IN THE BOX AND MRS. ROACH ALLEGEDLY GRABBED HIS RIGHT HAND AND SANK HER TEETH INTO IT. IN FELONY COURT TODAY, MRS. ROACH'S ATTORNEY ARGUED THAT HIS CLIENT'S TEETH WERE FALSE AND COULDN'T HAVE DONE MUCH DAMAGE. MAGISTRATE NATHAN BUTTERFIELD DIDN'T SEE IT THAT WAY. HE SET BAIL AT 500-DOLLARS AND ORDERED MRS. ROACH TO STAND TRIAL ON CHARGES OF ASSAULT.

Example 2

STEP 1—SITUATION AND CHARACTER—LEAD:
WHAT STARTED AS A HELICOPTER TOUR OF MONTREAL, TURNED INTO A SCENE STRAIGHT OUT OF A COPS-AND-ROBBERS MOVIE.

STEP 2—RISING ACTION:
PILOT JOHN NEWCOMB CHARTERED HIS HELICOPTER TO A COUPLE FOR A TOUR OF THE CITY. BUT ONCE IN THE AIR HIS PASSENGERS

DEMANDED HE LAND AT OLYMPIC STADIUM WHERE THEY
TRANSFORMED THE CHOPPER WITH LETTERING INTO A POLICE
CHOPPER.

STEP 3—CLIMAX:
NEWCOMB SAID HE THEN WAS FORCED TO FLY THE COUPLE TO A
NEARBY SHOPPING CENTER WHERE HE SAT HANDCUFFED TO THE
CONTROLS WHILE THEY ROBBED THE ROYAL BANK.

STEP 4—FALLING ACTION:
THE ROBBERS RETURNED TO THE CHOPPER AND FORCED HIM TO FLY
THEM TO THE NEAREST SUBWAY STATION. THERE, NEWCOMB
MANAGED TO GET AWAY WHILE DODGING THREE SHOTS FROM HIS
EX-PASSENGERS.

STEP 5—DENOUEMENT OR OUTCOME:
POLICE CLOSED IN AND THE COUPLE SURRENDERED. THE BANK IS
REIMBURSING NEWCOMB FOR THE GASOLINE HE USED WHILE FLYING
THE ROBBERS.

Here is the story without the steps indicated.

WHAT STARTED AS A HELICOPTER TOUR OF MONTREAL, TURNED INTO
A SCENE STRAIGHT OUT OF A COPS-AND-ROBBERS MOVIE. PILOT JOHN
NEWCOMB CHARTERED HIS HELICOPTER TO A COUPLE FOR A TOUR OF
THE CITY. BUT ONCE IN THE AIR HIS PASSENGERS DEMANDED HE LAND
AT OLYMPIC STADIUM WHERE THEY TRANSFORMED THE CHOPPER
WITH LETTERING INTO A POLICE CHOPPER. NEWCOMB SAID HE THEN
WAS FORCED TO FLY THE COUPLE TO A NEARBY SHOPPING CENTER
WHERE HE SAT HANDCUFFED TO THE CONTROLS WHILE THEY ROBBED
THE ROYAL BANK. THE ROBBERS RETURNED TO THE CHOPPER AND
FORCED HIM TO FLY THEM TO THE NEAREST SUBWAY STATION. THERE,
NEWCOMB MANAGED TO GET AWAY WHILE DODGING THREE SHOTS
FROM HIS EX-PASSENGERS. POLICE CLOSED IN AND THE COUPLE
SURRENDERED. THE BANK IS REIMBURSING NEWCOMB FOR THE
GASOLINE HE USED WHILE FLYING THE ROBBERS.

ASSIGNMENTS: WRITING THE FIVE-STEP NEWS STORY

1. As before, use a newspaper or a newspaper wire service as your
news source.
2. Select and clip stories from these sources for each of the following
types: local, state, regional, national, international.

3. Mount each clipping on an $8\frac{1}{2}$-×-11-inch sheet of typing paper. Be sure the sheet is identified with your name, class, date, and the nature of the specific assignment.

4. Work out a detailed fact sheet from each clipping.

5. Review the definition for each step in the Five-step Process and write your story step by step.

6. Be sure to turn in the following: a copy of your source material; a copy of your fact sheet; a step-by-step copy of your Five-step news story; a copy of your story without the steps indicated.

CHAPTER **5**

Word
Watching

WORDS THAT COMMUNICATE INADEQUATELY

For writers who want to triumph over illiteracy and unintelligibility, the following information about words should be helpful. These examples of usage and misusage are from network and regional stations.

Although anyone may misuse words, the repetition of a mistake can break down the quality of language communication and decrease its effectiveness. Misuse also limits a writer's ability.

Because success with words depends largely on the willingness and determination of the user, here are some specific ways to control the use of certain troublesome words found in newswriting.

Adjectives and Adverbs

An excessive use of adjectives and adverbs in writing for radio and television will tend to turn the message into a combination of exaggerations, value judgments, and personal opinions. Adjectives and adverbs should be used sparingly because exaggerations, value judgments, and personal

84

opinions are attitudinal and indicate more about the writer than about the subject being described. Adjectives and adverbs indicate how the writer feels about something, or how he or she sees something. For example, when you say, "It's a nice day," you are indicating how you feel about the day, not how the day really is.

How to correct this writing habit? First, remember that a day is not likely to seem nice to the receiver of the message if he has a physical or mental pain. Also, too many things can be nice. The best way to correct the habit of using adjectives and adverbs excessively is to omit them until you discover how to use those that are specific for a particular occasion and for that occasion only.

Adjectives

An adjective is used to modify a noun. Therefore it must *denote a specific quality* of the thing being named, not a quality you impose upon it. In addition, that same adjective should rarely be used to modify another noun. For example: pretty good, pretty bad, pretty steep, pretty deep, pretty dumb, etc., are examples of opinion and tell nothing factual about the condition being described.

Note how the meaning in the following sentences becomes more specific by removing the adjectives.

1. The governor won the race by a huge margin of ten thousand votes. (Omit huge.)
2. The truck he was driving had monstrous oversized tires on it. (Omit monstrous and on it.)
3. The senator served the greatest, tastiest fish sandwich ever. (The senator served a tasty fish sandwich.)
4. The police found the house chock-full of marijuana. (The police found the house filled with marijuana.)
5. The phony repairmen were offering the most personalized service of any in town. (Rewrite.)

Adverbs

An adverb is a word used to modify a verb, adjective, or another adverb. An adverb expresses a relationship of manner, quality, time, place, degree, number, denial, opposition, affirmation, or cause. An adverb is frequently recognizable because of its *ly* ending. The use of adverbial phrases often clutters and confuses messages, and therefore the understanding of the listener-viewer. Adverbs often express a prejudiced point of view.

Here are samples that illustrate problems some writers have with adverbs.

1. The governor was overwhelmingly reelected. (The governor was reelected by a majority.)
2. The player was grossly overweight. (Omit grossly.)
3. The governor is vastly more popular this term. (Omit vastly.)
4. He is diametrically opposed to the measure. (He is opposed to the measure, or He opposes the measure.)
5. He was clearly the better man. (Omit clearly.)
6. The opponent grudgingly conceded the election. (Omit grudgingly.)

The I, Me, My Habit

Another habit in which even professionals indulge is the misuse of "I," "me," and "my." Learn how to use these three pronouns and you'll write better and have more fun doing it. Here are some misuses heard on network broadcasts.

1. If there ever was a fan it's me. (Use I instead of me.)
2. Fascinating! Maybe that's why I married a woman two years older than me. (Use I instead of me.)
3. The governor and myself will arrive at seven tonight. (Use I instead of myself.)
4. My job requires me to work weekends. (Rewrite and use my working, or that I work.)
5. Send your letter to myself in care of this station. (Use me instead of myself.)

Due to, Caused by, Because of

Whenever you can, use "caused by" or "because of" to replace "due to," without distorting the meaning. Note the following:

1. The plane was due to arrive at four in the afternoon. (This is a simple case of being redundant. The plane was scheduled, therefore it was due at four in the afternoon. Omit either to arrive, or due.)
2. His death was due to cancer. (No, his death was not scheduled. His death was caused by cancer, or Cancer was the cause of his death.)
3. Many homes in western Centerville were without electricity for two hours last night due to a blown transformer. (Use because of.)

These are the easiest ways to correct such errors. There are several ways that each might be rewritten.

Less and Fewer

The confusion around these two words is responsible for an error that is heard daily. To use these two words correctly, select "less" when referring to the degree of something. Use "fewer" when you are writing about things you can count. For example:

1. There were less people attending the concert Monday night. (Use fewer.)
2. You will gain fewer pounds if you eat less fat. (Correct.)

Humans vs. Human Beings

Another usage creeping into the language is the use of "humans" for "human beings." The word human is an adjective. It becomes a noun only when you write, "Human understanding is sometimes faulty," or "Human welfare doesn't always work." Because the word human is an adjective, its purpose in language is to identify what kind of being you are talking about: "They are human beings." "They are human beings and should be treated as such." "Human understanding is sometimes faulty." "Human welfare doesn't always work."

Many human beings who write for listener-viewers indulge themselves illogically in the formation of plural endings. For example, some plurals are formed by adding an s to a singular noun. But not all. A few of the hundreds of acceptable plurals formed in this way are:

teacher—teachers
tree—trees
boy—boys

But the plural of the adjective human has not until recently been used to create a plural noun, "humans." The plural has been "beings." Perhaps some writers thought the rule for turning words into plurals was universally applicable. As a result the adjective human was turned into a noun, humans, by adding an s. These writers forget that our language is not logical. For example, the plural of mouse is mice, and the plural of louse is lice, but the plural of spouse is not spice, at least in language.

To, Too, Two

Another usage that befuddles many beginning writers is that these three words, although pronounced the same, have three different meanings. The only way to clarify this confusion is to learn the meaning of each. Here is an example of correct usage: "It takes *too* long *to* get *to* Chicago driving *two* miles an hour."

Worditis

Worditis afflicts most beginning writers. Its symptom is easily recognized— excessive words. The cure for worditis is brevity. The writer accomplishes this by leaving out all words that are not needed.

When you become a professional writer you will discover there are many ways of handling words. There are words just for friends, words for formal occasions, in fact, words for every need and purpose. One set of words will not serve your every need.

To discover how words may be used for a specific purpose, begin by getting rid of all those that are in excess. Here are a few examples of worditis with suggestions for controlling it.

1. We call it an exceptionally new idea. (It is a new idea.)
2. It doesn't quite . . . (Omit.)
3. What I mean is . . . (Omit.)
4. Needless to say . . . (Why bother, then, if it is needless?)
5. Never forget . . . (Use remember . . . always be positive.)
6. And frankly to make an observation . . . (My opinion is . . .)
7. The Braves have won their last four games in a row. (The Braves won their last four games.)
8. There were no undue injuries to the players. (Really? What does undue mean? Unexpected?)

Short Forms

Never write over the listener-viewer's head. Instead, write so that you talk with each listener-viewer, not to and not at several. When you "talk" with an individual you generally use certain contractions. For example:

1. You've, for you have.
2. You're, for you are.

At no time should you write "your" when you mean "you are." Many beginning writers confuse the meaning of "your" with "you're."

On occasion, to avoid stilted word usage, you will write:

1. My name's . . .
2. They're here . . .
3. If you'd . . .
4. It's all . . .

But never go so far as to say "s'pose" for "suppose." A general rule to follow is, if a short form in a message calls attention to itself, it should be considered disruptive. Disruptive short forms should not be used.

Pronoun Reference

"His" and "him" confuse even many leading newswriters. "His" is a pronoun that denotes possession. His hat. His country. We're listening to his talk. When I think of his crossing the river at night in that small boat, I shudder.

Instead of the possessive pronoun "his," many writers blithely type the objective pronoun "him." This is an error because the act of crossing the river is his. His crossing—the same as it is his hat.

You can keep this confusion between "his" and "him" to a minimum if you will examine the experience you are talking about. This is how to do that. When you want the listener-viewer to hear what a man has to say in a speech, you say, "Listen to his speech." But when you want the listener-viewer to hear the speed at which he is speaking, or the way he combines words, or even the way he combines words and ideas, you say, "Listen to him!" If you consult a reputable grammar text you will find that "his" is in the possessive case. "Him" is in the objective case.

The same problem exists with the two words "me" and "my." You should say, "Listen to me when I speak," if you want us to give you our undivided attention. But you must say, "Listen to my speech," when you want us to focus our attention on what you have to say.

Pronoun references are a problem for most beginning writers. Apparently, using a pronoun reference and getting it to agree correctly is not easy because professional writers of all levels of society and education misuse pronoun references. Examples of such misuse can be heard on all the networks. Newspapers are filled with this misuse, as are the utterance and writing of governmental officials and leading educators.

Effort to promote the equality of the sexes is thought by some to be responsible for the increased confusion that haunts many writers who habitually use a plural pronoun to refer to a singular subject. If you are being grammatically illiterate because you are worried about discriminating against the sexes, there are several solutions.

One solution is to bravely use "him" as it has been used since the study of grammar first began. Another way is to write "him or her." Another way, and perhaps the best, is to be more specific. Instead of being illiterate when you write,

> EVERYONE SHOULD TAKE THEIR VOTING PROBLEMS TO THEIR
> CONGRESSMAN

recast the sentence to read:

> ALL VOTING CITIZENS SHOULD TAKE THEIR VOTING PROBLEMS TO
> THEIR CONGRESSMAN.

(Now you have a plural with a plural.)

There are other ways to write this sentence. For example:

> EVERY CITIZEN HAS A RIGHT TO REFER VOTING PROBLEMS TO HIS
> REPRESENTATIVE IN CONGRESS.

(Or her, but not their.)

Each change is grammatically correct, and the change adds variety to the writer's style.

There are many, many ways to express an idea. If you prefer to use everyone, then use the singular pronoun, either his or her, instead of the plural their.

Here are a few television misuses of various pronoun references. As you read them remember that singular nouns require singular pronouns. Collective nouns also require singular pronouns. For example:

1. In a democracy everyone has a right to express their opinion. (Use an, his, her, or rephrase sentence.)

2. The average individual respects the wishes of the group because they hate to be considered odd. (Instead of they use he, she, or rephrase sentence.)

3. Everyone wants to look their best. (Instead of their use her, his, or rephrase sentence.)

4. The court also declined to consider their ruling that police warrants were valid. (Instead of their use its.)

5. A person can never be too careful about their use of language. (Instead of their use her, his, the, or rephrase sentence.)

6. I'd be worried about him getting to the quarterback. (Instead of him use his or the person's name.)

7. When the earthquake happened everyone thought their furnace had blown up. (Instead of their use his, her, or rephrase sentence.)

8. Nobody can break tackles better than him. (Instead of him use he, or use person's name.)

9. Everybody has their own job to do. (Instead of their use his, her, or a.)

10. Charleston, South Carolina, is having their Spoleto Festival. (Instead of their use its.)

Was and Were

These two verbs seem to give many beginning writers a lot of trouble, and they also seem to bother many professional writers. Perhaps the reason for this is that when the writers were young, misusing these two words was ingrained. We are often the product of our environment. For example, the following incident was on television news. A teacher took fourteen high school students from a law course to witness a court proceeding concerning a judge's right to carry a gun. The trial involved a defendant who had rushed the judge. The judge pulled out a gun and threatened to shoot the attacker if he didn't restrain himself.

When asked her opinion by a reporter, the teacher praised the judge's gun policy and said, "If I was a judge, I'd carry a gun too."

By her use of was for were this teacher is continuing to reinforce the illiterate usage by her students.

As a beginning writer, fix in mind this fact about was and were. For any condition that is untrue, contrary to fact, always write were. The teacher should have said were (contrary to fact): "If I were a judge, I'd carry a gun too." She is not a judge.

Redundancies

Mention was made of the tendency of many radio and television writers to be wordy. Writers should learn to state concepts without being redundant. There is no time for wordy newswriting. Yet many broadcast stations, both radio and television, continue to turn off listener-viewers by talking too much and saying too little. Naturally we are not talking about purposeful redundancy.

The following are redundancies taken from actual broadcasts. Note how repetitious they are. The correct usage is in italics. For example, why say, "absolutely certain." If you are certain, or sure, that is enough. There is no degree of certainty. The same holds for advanced preparation. Doing something in advance is what preparation means—ahead of time. For example:

1. all *complete*
2. all *unanimous*
3. annual *birthday*
4. *auction* sale
5. *bouquet* of flowers
6. *canceled* out
7. completely *engulfed*
8. *knots* an hour
9. local *neighborhood*
10. most *unique*
11. new *construction*
12. *consensus* of opinion
13. *empty* space
14. *endorse* on the back
15. *equal* to one another
16. final *verdict*
17. past *history*
18. *refer* back
19. *talking* aloud
20. totally *abolished*

There are hundreds of these redundancies to be avoided.

Compared to and Compared with

1. When two objects or things of the same order are brought together to note their likeness or their difference, the word compared should be followed by with (compared with).

2. When two objects or things are of a different order, the word compared should be followed by to (compared to).

When a writer is having with and to problems, he/she may achieve greater clarity by rewriting the sentence and omitting the comparison combination. Note the following sentences. The correct usage is given in parentheses.

1. Boys, when compared to girls, make more sex-appropriate responses. (Use with to note their differences. They are of the same order. But the sentence should be rewritten. For example: Boys show greater sex-appropriate responses than girls.)

2. When the present city is compared to its pre-World War II status, vast differences are noted. (Use with to note the differences. Rewriting will also help clear up the fuzzy thinking.)

3. Going to a dance was much more enjoyable compared to going to a movie. (Rewrite: Going to a dance is more enjoyable than going to a movie.)

4. The high school senior test scores this year when compared to the senior test scores last year are higher. (with)

5. The prices of clothes today when compared to the prices in the 1940s are sky high. (with)

6. Ted Kennedy's voice has been compared with the noise made by an earth mover. (to)

7. Liberated women, compared to unliberated women, are a threat to men and their masculinity. (with)

8. The acting ability of Ronnie Howard has been compared to that of John Wayne. (with)

9. Dave Parker's batting performance may be compared to that of Reggie Jackson's. (with)

That and Which

Knowing when to use that and when to use which is essential to a writer. When used correctly, that introduces a restrictive clause. Which is used to introduce a nonrestrictive clause. In this way two different ideas are created. Accordingly, at no time should the information introduced by that be set off from the rest of the sentence by commas because it is essential to the meaning of the sentence.

However, the information introduced by which must always be set off by commas from the rest of the sentence to indicate that the basic thought is complete without the which clause.

Note how the use of that and which is differentiated in the following sentences:

1. We repeat responses which are rewarding. (Use that, not which.)
2. We define a stimulus as anything which the organism has the capacity to perceive, to sense. (Use that, not which.)
3. Each of the following sentences has a different meaning. The difference is determined by whether that or which is used, which affects how the sentence is punctuated.
   a. The ladder that is broken is in the garage. (Correct)
   b. The ladder, which is broken, is in the garage. (Correct)
4. This is the truck which ran over the dog. (Use that, not which.)
5. Charges of physically injuring Miss Jones that would have called for life imprisonment without parole were dropped. (Use which instead of that and place a comma after Jones and before were.)
6. Their football team that was undefeated all last year lost all but one game this season. (Use which instead of that and insert a comma after team and before lost.)
7. The dispute is over the salt water canals which were filled in by the state. (Use that instead of which.)
8. Diatribe is a form of writing which may be delightful but is seldom convincing. (Use that instead of which.)
9. Inducements that are not needed or are offered inappropriately may block the effects of other inducements. (Correct.)

Note that occasionally which is used in preference to that when the writing is formal, as in the sentence found in the Bible: "Let us now go even unto Bethlehem; and see this thing which has come to pass." In this case it was probably used by the translators to break up the repetitious sound of "th." Without the which there would have been three "th" sounds in a row, which adds to the problem of speaking it aloud.

The careful writer who wishes to develop precision and specificity of style will always go which-hunting, as E. B. White put it, for the purpose of improving his or her style even though it may often mean recasting the sentence.

NAME–CALLING WORDS

Certain words have acquired negative connotations. As a result you may have a problem, even when you use them accurately, in communicating the intended meaning without distracting the listener-viewer's concentration.

Therefore, as long as certain words are used to name call, belittle, or verbally punch someone in the nose, the newswriter will need to substitute other words or add words to limit the meaning. For example, instead of saying, "He's a southerner," or "Yankee," it is possible to write, "He's from the state of ———," or "He's from [town]," without disrupting the listener-viewer's concentration.

The following words may belittle human identity, dignity, and reputation, depending on their context. Every successful newswriter uses them with care.

activist	Christian way	establishment
addict	chubby	fag
alkie	chump	fairy
ambulance chaser	cool cat	fanatic
American way	Commie	fascist
beatnik	Communist inspired	freak
bellhop	conservative	freeloader
bigmouth	cop	free thinker
big wheel	coward	fuzz
binge	cracker	gang
boozer	creep	goof
broad	damn Yankee	gook
bully	deadbeat	grease monkey
bum	democracy	half-baked
busybody	dictator	head shrinker
capitalist	ding-dong	hero
chauvinist	drunkard	hick
cheap	dude	hillbilly
chick	dummy	hippie

homo	party pooper	sissy
hoodlum	permissive	skinny
hooker	pervert	slacker
housewife	pig	slob
hamburger joint	pinko	slow
idiot	pit	slum
industrialist	playboy	snitch
janitor	politician	snob
jerk	polluted	sophisticated
Jesus freak	pseudo	soused
jittery	punk	southerner
jock	quack	square
joint	queer	straight
junkie	racist	stripper
kook	radical	stupid
libber	reactionary	sucker
liberal	rebel	swindler
liar	red	sympathizer
left-wing	redneck	tax-dodger
lesbian	rearguard	teen-ager
loser	revolutionary	terrorist
loudmouth	ringleader	thing
mamma's boy	rookie	turkey
miser	sadist	twit
mob	savage	Uncle Tom
moocher	segregationist	uncouth
narc	sexist	undertaker
news manager	shady	vain
nitwit	show-off	wino
nut	shrink	worldly
nympho	shyster	Yankee
ox	sinner	yardman

Name-calling words are colorful and often vivid. However, words with a quieter emotional tone are often substituted for the original concept in newswriting. In the following list the name-calling word is followed by a second word that is often used as a substitute. This substitution helps ease the reality that is associated with the name-calling word. In newswriting you find yourself on occasion searching for the less realistic word, whereas a specialty writer might use the name-calling word deliberately.

breast—bosom, chest	charity case—welfare recipient
bull fighter—matador	constipation—irregularity
butt—posterior	cook—chef

crazy—mentally deranged	mick—Irishman
crippled—handicapped	midget—short person
dead—deceased	old people—elderly
death notice—obituary	overdose—too many pills
died—passed away	pig—officer
drunk—intoxicated	rape—sexual assault
fat—overweight	retarded—[children] with
frog—Frenchman	special needs
garbageman—sanitation worker	second-hand—preowned
grave—last resting place	senile—absent minded
graveyard—cemetery	shrink—psychiatrist
grease monkey—mechanic	stink—odor
janitor—custodian	sweat—perspire
kicked out—discharged	throw up—regurgitate
libber—feminist	toilet paper—bathroom tissue
loose—immoral	toilet—commode
lower class—across the tracks	wop—Italian
mailman—postman	

USING WORDS WE HEAR BUT DON'T SEE

The fact that meanings are in people and not in the words they hear becomes evident when we discover that a word frequently means one thing to one person and something quite different to another. As a result of these differences some words take on strange connotations.

For example, the word enormity is used by many writers to describe the size of an object. During a recent *National Geographic Report*, "Invincible World," the narrator referred to "the enormity of the sky," when he obviously was describing its vastness.

The standard meaning of enormity is "immoderateness," "outrageousness," or "great wickedness." Only the words enormous, enormously, and enormousness refer to that which is extraordinarily large or gigantic.

Many highly paid writers use words inaccurately because they do not know the meanings of words they define within their own frame of reference. For example, a comedian in his routine explained that he thought his brother's name was "Dammit" because that is what his parents always yelled at him when they wanted his attention.

Another example of misplacing a meaning is the phrase "taken for granted." It is a phrase that many individuals hear and use as they grow up, yet do not spell correctly when they write it. Apparently they misspell it because the dialect in their community did not differentiate adequately between the sound of *d* and the sound of *t*. As a result, many heard the word granted as granite. Later when that person uses the expression in a written message, it is written "taken for granite."

The following words are often unintentionally misused:

1. compromise for comprise
2. refrain for restrain
3. dislocate for disassociate
4. defends for contends
5. precedings for proceedings
6. one day for some day, or sometime
7. acclaimed for demonstrated

Every newswriter should consult a dictionary and know the specific meanings for each of the following pairs of words.

1. block—bloc
2. bus—buss
3. careen—crash
4. comprise—compose
5. compliment—complement
6. cost—price
7. create—establish
8. engine—motor
9. flier—flyer
10. lady—woman
11. take—bring
12. locate—situate
13. man—gentleman
14. lure—entice
15. original—initial
16. police—policemen
17. stationery—stationary
18. verbal—oral—aural
19. revolver—pistol
20. cartridge—bullet—shell

CONTROLLING SINGLE- AND MULTIPLE-MEANING WORDS

The newswriter can increase his or her ability to communicate by avoiding words that seem specific when used in person-to-person conversation, but are not clear when written to be spoken on radio or television. Also, some words are better left in the dictionary. And of course it is obvious that words with single meanings are easier to use than are words with multiple meanings. However, many words with multiple meanings must of necessity be used from time to time. The problem with multimeaning words is to limit their meanings. For example, the word building means many things about a construction. Therefore, when that word is used its meaning must be limited. The word igloo and the word wigwam each mean just one kind of building. Furthermore, igloo and wigwam are each words with a single, specific meaning.

Neither the listener-viewer nor the writer has the identification problem with a single meaning word that each has with a multiple meaning word. Single meaning words usually designate and identify places and things. As such they generally need less limiting. Here are a few examples. There are many others in the dictionary.

avocado	lyre
bicycle	peanut
clarinet	reindeer
forehead	skateboard
grapefruit	sunglasses

Words with multiple meanings must have their meanings limited by the use of an additional word or words. But even when the meaning is limited in this way the writer should avoid using the same multiple meaning word more than once in the same sentence. It is even better to avoid using it more than once in a paragraph when its use may be confusing. For example, note how meaning becomes confused and diffused in the following sentence when the word call is used: Jack's call to Harry told him to call Bert to give his roommate a calling down for calling up at midnight and calling him a liar for calling off the date.

Consult any unabridged dictionary and you will find there are approximately forty different usage definitions for the multimeaning word call.

Thousands of words in our language are considered to have multiple meanings. To illustrate the problem a newswriter faces when having to use multimeaning words, here are a few definitions for the word fast.

1. A friend is fast when he is loyal.
2. A watch is fast when it is ahead of time.
3. A person is fast when he or she can run rapidly.
4. A racetrack is fast when it is in good running condition.
5. A fast may be a period of noneating.
6. A ship is fast when it is tied with its mooring lines.
7. A person is fast when he is tied down.
8. A person is fast when he or she moves in immoral company.
9. Colors are said to be fast when they do not run.
10. Some people like to play fast and loose.
11. To be fast asleep is to be deep in sleep.
12. To be fast by is to be near.
13. Photographic film is fast when it is sensitive to light.
14. Bacteria are fast when they are insensitive to antiseptics.

CONTROLLING MULTIMEANING WORDS WITH SYNONYMS

Perhaps the most successful way to control a word that has several meanings is to use a synonym. All newswriters struggle with this problem.

Sportswriters find it especially useful to develop a large vocabulary of substitute words, or synonyms, for multimeaning words. Read the sports section of a newspaper and listen to top sportscasters. As an example, here are some basic synonyms that can be used to replace the verb defeated. Consult your dictionary and thesaurus for others.

bashed	outshown	topped
battered	raked	toppled
bested	ripped	trampled
blasted	sank	trimmed
clipped	scalped	tripped
crushed	shaved	triumphed
downed	skinned	trounced
lashed	slashed	vanquished
mangled	slaughtered	walloped
mashed	slipped	whipped
massacred	smothered	whitewashed
mauled	squeezed	
nicked	stifled	

Most synonyms are classifiable either as verbs or as nouns. Therefore meanings will vary in terms of whether the word stands for a person, place, or thing (a noun) or whether the meaning denotes action (a verb). Note the different verb and noun meanings in the following synonyms.

1. beef—complain, cow, bull, steer, meat, grumble, lament
2. chair—head, rule, lead, seat, place, bench, helm, control
3. circle—ring, girdle, encompass, clique, band, orbit, friends
4. dough—money, green, cash, loot, bread, bucks, funds, wealth
5. flame—sweetheart, blaze, fire, passion, zeal, love, emotion
6. foul—dirty, stormy, unfair, obscene, bad, ugly, base, vicious
7. free—liberated, unrestrained, uninhibited, complimentary
8. hamper—hinder, impede, basket, bassinet, container, obstruct
9. handle—feel, grip, direct, operate, touch, manage, manipulate
10. high—drunk, luxurious, tainted, lofty, towering, good, foul
11. left—leave, remaining, residual, abandoned, sinister, alone, port
12. match—contest, pit, bout, marriage, similar, equal, retaliate
13. nag—demand, horse, quarrel, pester, badger, importune
14. pitcher—jug, ewer, vase, urn, one who throws a baseball
15. police—bull, cop, copper, fuzz, heat, officer, patrol
16. pop—snap, crack, burst, explode, break, noise, unexpected, soda, father
17. railroad—force, pressure, push, train, method, expedite
18. rate—price, cost, judge, score, evaluate, price, estimation

19. ring—encircle, girdle, encompass, toll, chime, resound, gang
20. ruler—president, dictator, governor, authority, straightedge
21. run—dash, manage, scoot, direct, sprint, bolt, flee, hurry
22. ship—vessel, craft, deliver, mail, send, boat, gig, raft
23. spin—twirl, whirl, rotate, gyrate, reel, journey, exaggerate
24. spring—leap, bound, release, reveal, disclose, season, source
25. state—estate, say, case, mood, aver, express, area of a nation
26. stir—move, budge, incite, provoke, agitate, excite, fuss, jail
27. squash—smash, flatten, destroy, obliterate, crush, vegetable, sport
28. tan—cure, sunburn, thrash, beige, color, henna, auburn, spank
29. tear—rip, tatter, break, dash, rampage, violence, spree
30. traffic—trade, transportation, deal, movement, truck, commerce

The ambitious writer will find many other synonyms for each of the thirty words just listed. Every newswriter should develop a ready reference notebook of his or her favorite multimeaning words. These words can be found in any unabridged dictionary and reputable thesaurus. The problem with leaving them in these books until needed is that it takes too much time to find them when you're in a hurry. Sometimes you will need to look in eight or ten sections to really get the job done. Building yourself an alphabetized ready reference also has the advantage of developing the imagination.

CHAPTER **6**

Newswriting Techniques

TRANSITIONAL WORDS AND PHRASES

A single statement is rarely able to communicate a message satisfactorily to every listener-viewer. To become a satisfactory message, most single statements need help. They need the assistance of additional information. For example, the following single statement needs such help:

A FIRE IS REPORTED TO BE OUT OF CONTROL IN THE HILLS OVERLOOKING LOS ANGELES.

That statement says what is happening. A fire is out of control. It also tells where it is happening. But it does not satisfy the listener-viewer's complete need for information about the fire. As a single statement it needs additional information that helps answer the questions, "How did the fire start?" "Why is it out of control?" "Why hasn't it been put out?" and many others.

Answers to these questions will not be satisfactory unless they are carefully linked to the original statement and to each other through the use of what are known to professional writers as transitional words and phrases. It is this relationship through linking that helps facts and statements fulfill their function in a message. For example, note the underlined phrases in the following story:

A FIRE IS REPORTED RAGING IN THE HILLS OVERLOOKING LOS ANGELES. <u>ONE REPORT SAYS</u> A FIFTY MILE AN HOUR WIND IS CAUSING MOST HOMES IN THE AREA TO IGNITE LIKE KINDLING WOOD. <u>ANOTHER REPORT SAYS</u> THE FIRE IS OUT OF CONTROL BECAUSE OF NARROW ROADS AND INADEQUATE FIRE FIGHTING EQUIPMENT. <u>ALTHOUGH ARSON IS SUSPECTED</u>, THE CAUSE OF THE BLAZE IS STILL UNKNOWN.

After the opening statement, the writer links all the subsequent facts to it. All professional writers use transitional words and phrases for this purpose; they repeat, refer to, and parallel the basic statement. Note the number of words and phrases that help keep the listener-viewer's attention focused on the main subject, the fire.

Transitional words and phrases serve this function for all types of radio and television writing. They help one idea flow smoothly to the next. That is why the ability to use transitional words and phrases is an essential technique for you to acquire.

In addition to coordinating ideas, transitional words and phrases are used to improve the order and relationship of every idea a broadcast newswriter puts on paper. Their use helps produce:

1. A succinct unity that is coherent and essential in broadcast newswriting.

2. A clear and evident relationship between ideas from sentence to sentence.

3. A broader and more complete development in a longer story.

4. A comprehensiveness that contributes to a positive response from the listener-viewer.

Learning to use transitional words and phrases is easy. All the writer needs to do is discover how to identify them. They are already in his or her vocabulary. However, unless they are used accurately, most messages will fail to have adequate purpose and direction. That is why you should start putting transitional words and phrases to work for you immediately. Using them leads to singleness of purpose in everything you write. You will find their use limitless.

There are two basic kinds of transitional words and phrases: internal and external.

The Subject of a Sentence May Be Repeated

The subject of a previous sentence, the main word or group of words denoting that which is declared or stated, may be repeated in the sentence that follows. Repeating the noun turns it into an internal transition and is an ideal way to achieve emphasis by repetition. The following examples illustrate the usefulness of this technique:

1. ABC again took top honors in this week's Nielsen ratings. ABC relied heavily on reruns to maintain its top position.
2. The president is a good man. The president is a just man.
3. Bacon, eggs, and coffee make a perfect breakfast. Bacon, eggs, and coffee are as American as apple pie and mother.
4. This senior class achieved high scores on the S-A-Ts. This senior class is the best.
5. "Sixty Minutes" received top ratings last week. "Sixty Minutes" is a tough show to beat.
6. John Maxwell is a man you can count on. John Maxwell is a great leader.
7. Music appeals to more than man's ear. Music appeals to man's soul.
8. Professor Smith was worshiped by all his students. Professor Smith was the loneliest man I have ever known.
9. John Anderson was a leader. John Anderson was a man to remember.
10. Being young is the time to dream and discover. Being young is the best time of your life.
11. Running for some is a way to live. Running for some is a way to die.
12. That movie is the worst I have ever seen. That movie should be used as punishment.

The Central Idea or Key Word May Be Repeated

The writing technique for accomplishing this is to take the object of the first sentence, that which is being talked about, and use it as a subject in the second sentence. The noun equivalent in a verb construction may also be used. For example:

1. Legislators are arguing over a bill. The bill calls for higher university tuition.
2. The coach is taking a trip to Chicago. In Chicago he will interview several high school players.
3. The State Center for Children and Youth operates a program

designed to help victims of child abuse. Child abuse, a parental sickness, has become a major problem in America.

4. The telephone is a great convenience. It is a convenience that is greatly underrated by many people.

5. Everyone has in him some creativity. Creativity should be encouraged in everyone.

6. While putting the model together he exhibited great dexterity. His dexterity is an asset to his personality.

7. If you drink, don't drive. If you drive, don't drink.

8. Why do we need an education? An education will further our economic status.

9. The second baseman's throw was erratic. His erratic throw cost the team the game.

10. Intercollegiate athletics, we are told, foster good sportsmanship. Yet this good sportsmanship manifests itself in curious ways.

11. Education is the key to knowledge. Knowledge is the key to understanding and wisdom.

12. The issues that people think about are set by the media. Therefore, the media have a lot of impact.

A Pronoun Reference May Be Used as an Internal Transition

A pronoun is a word that is used instead of, or in place of, a noun. A pronoun is one of a small number of words referring to a person, place, or thing that is either named, asked for, or understood in the context of what is being written. The use of a pronoun reference as an internal transition is achieved by substituting a pronoun for the main noun in the second sentence. However, the relationship between the pronoun and its referent must be unmistakable. When the meaning is clear the pronoun reference as a writing technique may be used. For example:

1. Freud believed life is based on sex. He related everything we do to our hidden sexual drives.

2. The president is elected to serve a four-year term. He may be reelected to the presidency one more time.

3. Rich Little is a famous impersonator. He is also a famous comedian.

4. Clip that coupon. It may come in handy next time you go shopping.

5. Football is a tough sport. It requires that one be large and strong.

6. Rain is refreshing on a hot day. It cools the air.

7. A car is a form of transportation. It enables a person to be mobile.

8. The jet is one of the greatest conveniences. It saves people time and money in many ways.

9. Soon a cottage appeared in the distance. Its windows glowed in the darkness.

10. The best care comes from qualified dermatologists. They help thousands with visible results.

Parallel Structure

Parallel structure is a technique to improve the quality of your writing. It uses an idea in one sentence and then compares or contrasts it with another idea. A parallel structure is achieved by including in the second sentence a phrase structured similarly to the phrase used in the first sentence. Some of the ways that a parallel structure may be used can be seen in the following sentences:

1. He found acting in the theater inspiring. Acting in the movies was a bore.

2. The Chicago Cubs continue to lead their division. The Chicago White Sox continue to trail their division.

3. The economy of any state affects the economy of the United States. The economy of the United States affects the economy of the world.

4. Jogging helps strengthen your heart. Sitting around helps weaken it.

5. Some people rise to the top. Others tend to sink to the bottom.

6. A mirror is a reflection of reality. A magnifying glass is a distortion of reality.

7. The day is too short. The work is too long.

8. The phone keeps ringing, the kids keep crying, and I keep on going crazy.

9. When you eat too much you tend to gain weight. When you eat a little less than you need, you tend to lose weight.

10. Minutes pass slowly. Years pass quickly.

Enumeration

Enumeration as a technique to improve your writing employs the use of various counting devices. They are used for the purpose of achieving a smooth transition from one sentence to the next. As a writer you may develop enumerative devices by stating that there exists a particular number of items or events. Then you may count them one at a time, tell of or about one event after another, or give a listing item by item. The following sentences illustrate various ways that enumeration may be developed:

1. All the scoring was done in the first two innings. In the first, Farber belted a three-run homer. In the second inning, Jones lined a single that sent Farber home. That was the Braves' last run.

2. With one minute left, the Buccaneers trailed by seven. Thirty seconds later they had tied the score.

3. The bill has two faults. One, it's too expensive. Two, it doesn't have congressional support.

4. First, we must consider whether or not people actually want fluoridation of their water supply. Second, we must consider the cost of fluoridation.

5. This clarification was confusing for two reasons. First, he didn't state the problem. Second, he didn't explain it.

6. His new car has two energy sources. The primary source is gasoline. The second source is solar energy.

7. University students tend to eat two kinds of foods. Junk food is first, and sugar-based food is second.

8. Running does two things for me. First, it tones my muscles. Second, it works off my frustrations.

9. There are two reasons why I don't like that movie. One, it's too pornographic, and two, it's too violent.

10. You can solve your problem two ways. One, talk to the other person. Two, forget about it and hope he does too.

11. Men use three techniques for picking up women. First, there is the macho approach. Second, there is the nice guy approach. Finally, a man can use a hard-luck, sympathy act.

12. Our system of government is composed of three branches. First is the executive branch. Second is the legislative branch. Third is the judicial branch.

Addition

Addition as a writing device or technique is a means by which a thought may be expanded. The process uses certain words, or word combinations, with which to attach an additional meaning or thought unit to a previous one. The use of this process will help you supplement the main idea or thought.

The following words may be used to introduce or relate additional meanings (the serious writer will discover many more than those listed here):

again	and	consequently
along	another	continuous
also	besides	further

furthermore	likewise	subsequently
included	moreover	then
including	next	therefore
last	plus	too

The following phrases are often used by writers in developing supplemental thoughts and meanings:

added to	as well as
along the same	at the same time
an additional	equal importance
another important	in addition
another point	in conjunction with
another related	not only

The following sentences illustrate some of the many ways that addition as a technique may be used:

1. Another related point is that a sorority furnishes a girl away from home with a group of friends she might never have known.
2. Besides that, the following day had much more to offer.
3. Furthermore, the plans include a double-decker parking lot.
4. In addition to a sales tax, there will be a five-cent house tax.
5. In conjunction with the expected change, the bill may cost taxpayers less than was anticipated.
6. Moreover, you may add extra milk to the mixture to make it thinner.
7. The coach also wants to be included.
8. The rain brought flooding conditions that increased the town's already disasterous situation.
9. The striking truckers made employee relations their latest demand along with wage increases.
10. You can learn to dress like an influential businessman as well as increase your profits.

Clarification

As a writing technique, clarification employs the use of certain words singly and in combination to help make what is being talked about more easily and more clearly communicated. Clarification is the process of giving an example within a paragraph, or of making a reference to something that is similar. Clarification uses certain words and phrases for the purpose of additional explanation. This use is to help assure understanding and comprehension of the message.

The following words, word combinations, and phrases are often used by professional writers to introduce additional explanation for the purpose of clarifying a thought. There are many others.

an explanation of this	said in another way
as a matter of fact	specifically
by that is meant	that is
clearly	that is to say
evidently	this means
for example	this seems
for the purpose of understanding	to be more explicit
in essence	to be more precise
in explanation	to clarify
in fact	to demonstrate
in other words	to illustrate

The following sentences illustrate some of the ways that the principle of clarification may be used within a paragraph:

1. America needs to develop alternative sources of energy. For example, why not develop our vast coal supplies?
2. Brevity is the key to preciseness.
3. Clearly it is evident that he is in error.
4. Coal, in other words, could help this country weather the gasoline scarcity.
5. For example, a young child learns to behave according to how his parents respond to him.
6. In essence, the desert offers many forms of perishable and nutritious life.
7. Said another way, the restoration of this building has increased the property values surrounding it.
8. Specifically, this bill doesn't account for inflation.
9. This means that job interviewers today are looking for college seniors with higher grade point averages.
10. What that means is, the railroads must receive aid from the government or become obsolete.

Comparison and Similarity

As a writing technique, comparison and similarity employ the use of certain words to bring two or more objects, thoughts, persons, or events together within a paragraph. This is done for the purpose of noting their likenesses. The use of comparison and similarity as a writing technique helps clarify and/or emphasize resemblances.

The following words, word combinations, and phrases represent a few of the ways that comparison and similarity may be used:

also	in a similar way
analogous to this	in comparison
analogy	in the same way
a related point is	it is, moreover
as	keeping this in mind
comparatively	like
corresponding to this	like the previous point
equivalent	on the same note
identical	representative
imitation of	similar
in a like manner	similarly

The following sentences represent a few of the ways that comparison and similarity may be used:

1. In an analogy, the book is the door to knowledge.
2. The job demands a corresponding mastery of skills.
3. Speaker of the House O'Neill is now at odds with President Reagan.
4. The storm caused wreckage the like of which this town has never seen.
5. Like the novel, the movie focused on the main character's thoughts.
6. Like the coach, each member of the team has a mustache.
7. In many ways a dog is like a man. Each is sensitive to others.
8. There is no parallel to this kind of problem.
9. Compared to the old, this new management concept is more comprehensive.
10. In a similar way he is opposed to male chauvinism.

Contrast

As a technique in writing news, contrast employs the use of certain words and/or phrases to indicate the differences and dissimilarities between two or more objects, persons, thoughts, or events. The use of contrast as a writing technique within a paragraph is for the specific purpose of making differences clearer to the listener-viewer.

The following words, word combinations, and phrases represent a few of the many ways that contrast may be expressed:

after all	in spite of
although	instead of
at the same time	neither
but	nevertheless
conversely	notwithstanding
despite	on the contrary
dissimilarly	on the one hand
for all that	on the other hand
however	still
if not	unlike
in contrast	yet

The following sentences illustrate some of the ways that contrast may be used as a technique to clarify an idea:

1. Although he is younger than most, he has more experience.
2. The election was expected to favor the Liberal party, although it lost by a wide margin.
3. He ran the Boston Marathon as no other man had.
4. Despite this fact, the coach intends to go ahead with his regular game plan.
5. Salvador Dali's style is distinct among surrealist artists.
6. In spite of their differences, the two congressmen remained friends.
7. The senator's stand on the property rights issue marks him as the sole liberal in the Senate.
8. The documentary related the story of the press during the 1930s. Nevertheless, the story can be applied to our time.
9. On the other hand, money can create problems.
10. The coach still thought his quarterback did the best job.

Exemplification

As a writing technique, exemplification is produced by using a word, or a combination of words, to introduce an example or an explanation that will illustrate a previous statement. Exemplification as a technique increases clarity and comprehension.

The following words and word combinations represent a few of the ways that exemplification may be used as a writing technique:

a case in point	as the statement implies
as the author states	as the title reminds us
as the situation suggests	exemplifies

exhibits	the man testified
for example	the sign reads
for instance	the speaker declared
habit calls for	the speaker pointed out
he explained	the tapes revealed
indicates	this was expressed
in explanation	to exemplify
practice establishes	to extend
shows	to point out
the law demands	to relate to

The following sentences are examples of how the principle of exemplification as a writing technique may be used to develop clarification:

1. As the title indicates, this is a conference on sports medicine.
2. As the article discloses, the difficulties of city life are many.
3. The mistakes of the past, as represented by last year's defeat, will be corrected for this year's election.
4. Everyone knows his attitude typifies his upbringing.
5. Inflation is rampant in the gasoline industry. The high cost of gasoline exemplifies this point.
6. The story of Johnny Carson exemplifies what success can be.
7. For example, some social customs require that women be submissive.
8. It is perfectly clear that the bill draws the line on spending.
9. The speaker pointed out that as an interviewer he is looking for college seniors with a grade point average of three-point-five or better.
10. To point out a difference, this typography reflects a conventional quality, while that form reflects a contemporary quality.

Place

This writing technique involves the use of words and phrases that designate and create visual imagery. Place is achieved by using an appropriate noun, verb, adjective, adverb, or combination of words to explain the physical location of a person, place, object, occasion, circumstance, or context in relation to an event or situation.

The following words may be used in classifying idea relationships in terms of where and how:

above	among	at	beside
across	area	behind	between
after	around	below	beyond

by	inside	opposite	spot
centrally	midway	outside	there
elsewhere	near	past	underneath
everywhere	nearly	someplace	whereabouts
here	neighborhood	somewhere	within

The following phrases are especially useful for classifying relationships of place in terms of where and how:

across from	in the area
around the corner	in the vicinity of
away from	midway to
close by	nearby
close to	nearest to
far away	next to
here and there	on the farthest side of
in midstream	on the outside
in some place	over there

The following sentences illustrate ways that place as a technique in writing may be used:

1. Around town you might find many interesting and enjoyable activities.
2. Below the surface there are 40-million barrels of oil.
3. The plane was high above the clouds.
4. In what area of politics is he interested?
5. Inside his mind there are four personalities at work.
6. The bullet lodged near his spine.
7. Standing next to the congressman is his wife.
8. On the other side of the harbor, shrimp boats docked to unload their catch.
9. The car stopped just short of the cliff.
10. She is the third female assigned to that position in the city government.

Qualification

As a writing technique, qualification is used to modify an attribute, statement, concept, or idea, or to restrict the condition essential to understanding, accepting, or believing it. The use of such qualifying words or phrases helps the writer develop specificity. Qualification also clarifies a condition or state of being and helps the listener-viewer comply with it or satisfy a condition by understanding it.

When used appropriately, the following words help restrict or limit the meaning of an initial statement so that it is more readily understood. Qualification words are helpful in clarifying idea relationships in terms of why.

apparently	may be	presumably
clearly	obviously	seemingly
conceivably	perhaps	slightly
considering	plainly	somewhat
evidently	possible	unfortunately
hopefully	possibly	unique

Qualification phrases are especially useful in restricting or limiting the meaning of an initial statement. For example:

according to	in view of
as far as one can judge by appearance	it can be assumed that
based on	it can be inferred that
because of	it is equally true that
for certain	it is reasonable that
I am certain of	it may be that
I am sure that	logically speaking
I feel without a doubt	when everything is considered
in anticipation of	without a doubt

The following sentences illustrate some of the ways that the technique of qualification may be used:

1. Apparently the coach is not happy with his position.
2. Clearly everyone can see the senator's mistake.
3. Considering everything else, this creative strategy should meet our needs.
4. The game was embarrassing. Obviously the team needed more practice.
5. It can be assumed that the better student will make the better employee.
6. The senator said he would have to reconsider in view of the new evidence.
7. Finishing the plans for the new civic center may take longer than expected.
8. Apparently he is not the man for the job.

9. Without a doubt the black-and-white half-page spread is more cost efficient than the three-color half-page spread.

10. He will vote "yea" on the condition that his bill is supported.

Reference

As a writing technique, the use of reference means that the writer chooses a word, word combination, or phrase to point out a specified meaning. The use of reference as a writing technique also helps the writer call the listener-viewer's attention to a specific statement, passage, point, condition, circumstance, person, place, or thing. Reference is used to indicate how a statement or remark may have a bearing on the subject or problem being discussed.

The following words are useful in fulfilling a point of reference:

everyone	many	there	whatever
he	other	these	where
here	she	this	which
it	that	those	who

The following word combinations and phrases are often used by writers as reference:

associated with	relative to
concerned with	that which
everyone who	the one who
in accordance with	the person who
in reference to	the thing that
in the case of	with regard to
one that	

The following sentences illustrate some of the ways that reference as a technique may be developed:

1. The encyclopedia can be used to gather additional information.
2. Tom Brown is affiliated with the Lions Club.
3. Here are the names of all the members of the team.
4. His town has a small population.
5. The senator says he would like to see their material wants minimized.
6. This is a very important decision for the Senator.
7. In Montana it may be all right, but here it is unlawful.
8. Those, many scientists claim, are the symptoms of skin cancer.

9. Where we place our values reflects our personality.

10. Whatever the governor decides, the Senate and House will back him.

Summary

As a writing technique, summary is a means used to recapitulate, review, reexamine, reiterate, or sum up that which has been stated or implied. Generally the writer's use of the process is for the purpose of forming a conclusion in a concise and orderly fashion.

The following words are helpful to a writer who wishes to employ the technique of summary:

accordingly	briefly	hence
altogether	condensed	simply
basically	consequently	so
because	fundamentally	thus

The following phrases are often used by writers who wish to sum up or point out the significance of a statement in a succinct, summary fashion:

as a quick summary	in capsule	on the whole
as a reminder	in closing	to close
as a result	in conclusion	to recapitulate
in a few words	in review	to reiterate
in a nutshell	in short	to repeat
in brief	in summary	to sum up

The following sentences illustrate a few of the ways that summary may be used as a technique in the process of writing:

1. All in all, the race was successful.
2. Basically, the story concerns a young man's life.
3. The movie was supposed to be a romantic comedy.
4. Briefly, he believes his plan will work.
5. In a nutshell, the company needs more money.
6. In brief, he died of cancer.
7. In closing, remember to study now and party later.
8. In short, the Senator is in favor of utilizing the abundance of coal we have.
9. To sum up, the entire performance was excellent.
10. In summary, all microphones should be turned off until the introductory music has been taped.

Time

The use of a word that indicates some relationship to time is a useful writing technique. A word referring to time defines or specifies the period during which something has taken or will take place. Such words imply a succession of events within a given period.

The following words, plus many others, are used to indicate that an element of time is correlated to what is being said:

after	lately	since
afterward	later	soon
before	meanwhile	subsequently
continually	next	temporarily
currently	now	thereupon
during	past	throughout
earlier	presently	today
finally	recently	until
formerly	shortly	while
immediately	simultaneously	yesterday
last		

Phrases that indicate time are particularly useful to a writer wishing to identify or describe various aspects of an event or occasion:

after a short time	from that time until now
after a while	identical moment
a short time ago	in the course of history
at last	in the future
at that time	in the past
at the same time	recently
at this moment	shortly after
before now	until then
continually	when it's over

The following sentences illustrate some of the ways in which time as a technique may be used:

1. Before the operation, he could hit as well as field.
2. Earlier, the fashion was to wear flare-legged jeans.
3. Incidentally, the Seabrook demonstration occurred at the same time a nuclear power plant accident occurred in Utah.
4. Later the fashion will change to a different style.
5. The matter will be discussed later.
6. Presently the fashion is to wear narrow, straight-legged jeans.

7. A patrolman was the first to arrive at the scene of the accident.

8. A short time ago, the newspaper raised its advertising space rates.

9. Soon the economy will shift to a recession.

10. Subsequently the river is expected to flood the valley if the rain doesn't stop.

EXTERNAL TRANSITIONAL WORDS AND PHRASES

There is a second way of using transitional words and phrases. This technique helps the writer systematically develop a logical flow of ideas and emotions from one paragraph to the next. This second process is called external transitional words and phrases. By using external transitions you can avoid opening each succeeding paragraph repetitiously and monotonously. Variation helps retain the listener-viewer's interest.

External transitions also help the listener-viewer better understand the meaning of each new idea that is introduced. They serve this purpose because they are to the listener-viewer what street signs are to a nonresident looking for an address in a strange city. They point the way.

There are several techniques for making external transitions.

Key Words

Key words from one paragraph may be repeated in the first sentence of the succeeding paragraph. For example:

1. The final talk of the day ended without a disruption. But the disruptions provided by the citizens the next day in the small town of Quincy gave the candidate something he would never forget.

2. The bomb blast created chaos in the town. But the chaos subsided when the National Guard moved in.

3. The lecture series ended with a talk by Ralph Nader on consumer awareness. Consumer awareness is fast becoming a major issue to the American public.

4. The Blazers seemed to be having difficulty. But their real difficulty came later on in the game.

5. The demands of the rubber unions are threatening production. Discussion of these demands is currently underway.

6. The singles match was very exciting. This excitement, however, did not carry over to the doubles play.

7. Authorities grabbed two pounds of heroin. The heroin, they were later to learn, was but part of another scheme the convicts were trying to carry out.

8. Inflation was a major issue in the election. Another issue, though, was soon to surface.

Summary–Prognostication

The opening sentence in a new paragraph may serve a double purpose. First it may summarize what has been said, or what has transpired, and then conclude with a prognostication, or a prediction of things to come. For example:

1. Although *Jaws* was a big success, other shark movies may not do as well at the box office.
2. Although the weather has been good for the past week, we can expect much more rain in the days to come.
3. At the same time that OPEC raised its prices, measures were being taken by the U-S federal government to decrease the need for oil imports.
4. Credit cards may seem to be easy money, but some people are finding them less than desirable.
5. Drug abuse isn't just a problem among the lower class. Evidence from research indicates the problem is much more widespread.
6. Even though the veto will escalate inflation, other presidential actions will help the economy.
7. In view of the ongoing confrontation, efforts toward a cease-fire will evidently develop later.
8. Legislators feel the major concern is the budget, while the governor projects other problems.
9. The previous plays on mainstage have been so successful that a full house is expected opening night for the new play.
10. While the troops were marching toward the capital, rebel forces were forming within that city.

Subject Referral and Linkage

The subject matter of the previous sentence or sentences is referred to and then linked and related to the idea that is to be developed in the ensuing sentence. This writing technique, subject referral and linkage, is a useful device. For example:

1. A lot of bad effects can be attributed to drinking coffee. Tea drinking also has bad effects.
2. All in all, Clarice acted her part in the play like a professional. Another person who acted like a professional was Geoffrey.

3. Cowboy Billy Jones proved to be a "heck of a gambler." Most cowboys, including James West, were poor gamblers.

4. Considering all the facts, poodles have one of the highest degrees of intelligence among dogs. Another dog with a high degree of intelligence is the collie.

5. He was a great left-handed pitcher. When you mention left-handed pitching, however, there is no match for Sandy Koufax.

6. If you think Indian head nickels are rare coins to find, just wait until you try to find the 1948 silver dime.

7. The president vetoed all of Congress's proposals. Later that night, he did some proposing of his own.

8. Of all physical activities, jogging is very good exercise. However, another good form of exercise is swimming.

9. Explaining the behavior of animals is usually easy. Not so easy, however, is explaining human behavior.

10. All things considered, Macy's is a good choice for an unlimited selection of designer clothing. Another good choice for designer clothes is Rich's.

The Use of a Question as Linkage

The writer may ask a question at the end of a paragraph to help bridge the gap between two paragraphs. Theoretically the question is answered in the succeeding paragraph or paragraphs. When the subject is appropriate, a question may also be used as the opening to the new paragraph. The following sentences illustrate the use of a question as linkage:

1. Considering the slowness of weight loss, what foods are truly low in calories?

2. Because inflation seems to be uncontrollable, what controls can be imposed to halt rising prices?

3. Even with those adjustments, how can business still produce a profit?

4. How can the legislature deal with the problem?

5. If criminals can be rehabilitated, why are there so many repeat offenders?

6. The question before the Senate should be, Is there a solution?

7. The Cubs were considered contenders, but what of their opponents?

8. If the state of our economy continues to decline, will the President have a chance for re-election?

9. If the population of the world continues to grow, how long before we run out of room?

10. If Chicago rules against radar as a speed detector, how might that affect the rest of Illinois?

Enumeration

The use of enumeration as a technique may be internal, as previously defined and illustrated. However, enumeration may also be used as an external technique when it begins a paragraph. The amount of detail to be included determines whether enumeration should be used as an internal or as an external device. Each of the sentences below, without the paragraph that followed it, is an example of external transition:

1. Attraction to religious cults has roots in psychological needs. These include a desire for affection and a need for self-admiration.

2. An effective play depends on, one, realistic character interplay, and, two, indirect audience-character interaction.

3. Before purchasing a large item you need to, one, consider the quality of the product; two, consider the cost of the product; three, consider the warranty of the product if any; and four, compare the product with others of its kind.

4. The status of blacks has been improved by integration, new laws, and attitude change.

5. Fatigue can be caused by, one, lack of sleep; two, a bad diet.

6. Overexposure to the sun poses more for the sun bather than an appealing tan. It poses an increase in susceptibility to skin cancer and a tendency to wrinkle.

7. Memory comes from, one, the knowledge obtained; two, the sights we view; and three, our unconscious observations of life.

8. The Cubs need, one, a first baseman; two, a reliable third starter; and three, a new ball park.

9. There are various allurements to backpacking. These include back to nature fads and the challenge of nature itself.

10. For a TV production, a director considers, one, his need for appropriate placement of characters; two, good cameramen with acute skills; and three, good lighting engineers to create mood.

Changing Internal Words or Phrases into External Words or Phrases

Use of this technique does not limit your writing style for the reason that all internal transitional words and phrases classified under addition, classification, comparison, contrast, exemplification, place, qualification, reference, summary, and time may be converted into and used as external transitional writing devices.

Changing an internal word or phrase into an external device or writing technique is done by beginning the first sentence of the next paragraph with an internal word or phrase. This technique causes the internal word or phrase to serve in the capacity of an external transitional device. The following sentences, in which each statement is used to begin a new paragraph, illustrate the use of this shift as a writing technique:

ADDITION:

FURTHERMORE, THE LIBRARY HOLDS A STOREHOUSE OF KNOWLEDGE FOR ALL AGES.

FURTHERMORE, THE RULES FOR USING THE INTRICATE MACHINE ARE NECESSARY FOR THE MEN.

CLASSIFICATION:

BASICALLY, WHAT WE THEN HAD WAS A MIX-UP.

CLEARLY, THE PROGRAM NEEDS YOUR HELP NOW AND IN THE FUTURE.

COMPARISON:

LIKEWISE THE ITALIAN GOVERNMENT IS HAVING GASOLINE PROBLEMS.

KEEPING THIS PROBLEM IN MIND, IT SHOULD BE OBVIOUS WHICH COURSE OF ACTION TO CHOOSE.

CONTRAST:

IN SPITE OF THE RECENT GAS CRISIS, PEOPLE ARE DRIVING MORE.

ALTHOUGH GEORGE WASHINGTON IS THE FATHER OF OUR COUNTRY, LINCOLN IS THE MOST LOVED PRESIDENT.

EXEMPLIFICATION:

A CASE IN POINT IS THE TIME HE WAS ARRESTED FOR ASSAULT.

AS THE TITLE INDICATES, THE DOCTOR HAS INVESTED A LOT OF TIME IN HIS EDUCATION.

PLACE:

NEARBY, A POLICEMAN WAS RUNNING AFTER AN ASSAILANT.

BENEATH THE TREE, APPLES LITERALLY COVERED THE GROUND.

QUALIFICATION:

APPARENTLY THE HURRICANE HAD BEEN MORE DESTRUCTIVE THAN REPORTED.

IN VIEW OF THE COST, SEVERAL CONSIDERATIONS SHOULD BE WEIGHED.

REFERENCE:

THESE ARE SOME OF THE PROBLEMS WE FACE IN THIS COUNTRY.

WHILE SOME BELIEVE THE DRAFT IS NEEDED, OTHERS BELIEVE A RESUMPTION IS UNCALLED FOR AT THIS TIME.

SUMMARY:

IN OTHER WORDS, THE BLACKS ARE STILL BEING DISCRIMINATED AGAINST.

IN SHORT, WE CAN EXPECT THE COST OF GAS TO RISE.

TIME:

AFTERWARD, THE FIGHT BROKE OUT.

LATELY, HE HAS BECOME INDIFFERENT.

CHAPTER **7**

Specialty
Writing

SOCIAL ACCOUNTABILITY

Every broadcast news writer sooner or later is likely to become involved in some kind of specialty writing. This is a normal result of being a reporter who is alive and alert to what is happening in a coverage area. However, even with all the action available, specialty writing, like reporting, is not something one does without preparation.

Specifically a specialty writer must understand how to select information and turn it into writing that has in it the sounds and feelings and meanings that are present in an environment. All the writing skills and techniques you develop writing news are needed because the Commentary, Analysis, Editorial, Review, and Interview (C-A-E-R-I) each go one step further than reporting. This kind of writing, like investigative reporting, is a form of goal tending.

As a goal tender, the specialty writer's obligation is to bring social actions, needs, and responsibilities together and explain them. Functioning as a specialty writer is, therefore, a social responsibility, and most members of society avoid all aspects of social accountability outside their immediate needs because it requires an energy output beyond what

123

they are already giving.[1] Furthermore, by "not making waves," by "not meddling in somebody else's problem," many individuals feel they will be able to enjoy an existence that is free from worry.

This human characteristic, avoiding social accountability, is not new. As an attitude it has been present throughout the history of man. Be that as it may, the specialty writer's efforts, through the commentary, analysis, editorial, review, and interview, are needed to help listener-viewers understand and come to know their own social needs as well as those of others. Listen to the broadcasters who are doing this kind of writing on the networks. A few of them are Bill Moyers, Gene Shalit, John Chancellor, and those on "60 Minutes." There are others whose voices may be heard on local outlets.

SPECIALTY WRITING AND THE LISTENER-VIEWER

Much of today's formal oral-aural communicating, public speaking, and lecturing uses visible and audible symbols to gain an audience's attention and response. But the very nature of broadcast production confines and limits these communicating techniques. Radio depends entirely on confined audio. Television combines audio with visual but at the same time technically limits the use of each.

To add to that, the listener-viewer's environment itself may create reception distractions. For example, when the radio is on, the listener-viewer may be in a car on a noisy highway or in the stop-and-go traffic of a city. While the television is on, the listener-viewer may be in a bar or with members of the family performing household duties. The very nature of our environment tends to reduce listening and viewing to half-hearing and half-viewing. And yet, even under these distracting circumstances, concepts conveyed by broadcasting are responsible for many key attitudinal changes in society.

Cantril and Allport[2] were among the first to survey the effect of broadcasting on people. Since then many studies have measured listener-viewer responses. As a result of these surveys, we know that the nature and extent of listener-viewer attention is basically involuntary, because the listener-viewer is not required to listen or view. Instead, the listener-viewer focuses attention on the program because he or she feels emotionally compelled to turn on the set and listen or view.

In contrast to involuntary listening, attending a class and listening to a lecture is voluntary. Attending and listening are part of the contractual arrangement you agreed to when you signed up for the course.

[1] Dorothy Rethlingshafer, *Motivation as Related to Personality* (New York: McGraw-Hill Book Company, 1963).

[2] H. L. Cantril and G. W. Allport, *The Psychology of Radio* (New York: Harper and Row, 1935).

The broadcast specialty writer who combines the psychological principles found in voluntary listening and viewing with the psychological principles found in involuntary listening and viewing is frequently the more successful writer. Getting the listener-viewer to react both voluntarily and involuntarily is more easily accomplished when the writer incorporates the human factors of advantage.[3]

Change as an Attention Factor

Change is essential to keeping the listener-viewer's attention focused. Stated another way, a moving object is more interesting than a stationary one. The basic principle in all dramatic writing is that a stimulus can continue to move in a given direction and hold the attention only if the intensity of its direction is varied.

For example, in a commentary, analysis, editorial, review, or interview, the writer must alternate the importance of each remark made. This alternation is done by following a major statement with a medium or a minor statement, which in turn is followed by another major statement. This writing technique brings about a change in the intensity of content. When the content of a C-A-E-R-I consists of a series of events equal in importance, it will sound pompous, monotonous, if not dull. When such intensity without change dominates a writer's style, the listener-viewer is most likely to hit the radio or television off button.

However, when a series of statements is arranged in a varied pattern (a major, minor, major, medium, etc., order) and the specialty article is climaxed with a paragraph event or statement that develops an attention lift through humor or excitement, this use of change inevitably makes for better listening and viewing response.

It is generally believed that the television specialty writer has an advantage over the radio specialty writer. It is true that on television, change in the visual can be and is used as an attention technique. However, in the final analysis it is what the writer has to say and how he or she says it that makes the difference. Listen to network newscasters and you will see how change through writing is used as an attention factor.

Repetition as an Attention Factor

When repetition is used by a specialty writer as an element of style, it increases the listener-viewer's sensitivity to and awareness of what is being

[3] Bernard Berlson and Gary A. Steiner, *Human Behavior* (New York: Harcourt Brace, World, 1964). G. Murphy, *An Introduction to Psychology* (New York: Harper and Row, 1951).

communicated. Repetition is especially useful in any content that is heavy with facts. Its use helps comprehension and improves understanding. Naturally all repetition should vary in its use-technique.

The beginning specialty writer may not need additional repetition when following the Six-step and the Seven-step Processes. Repetition is present in the early steps of each of these. It occurs there for the purpose of catching and holding the listener-viewer's attention. It is also used to add clarification. Repetition through contrast is used in the latter steps of these processes. In addition, note the many repetition technique devices available in Chapter 6, "Newswriting Techniques."

Conflict as an Attention Factor

Every human concept or situation, whether positive or negative, has an inherent thesis, theme, or central idea that is directly or indirectly related to various problems, needs, feelings, or desires. This means that sooner or later someone will object or take issue with what is proposed or done.

That is the very meaning and nature of conflict. When a problem, need, feeling, or desire does not exist for someone, there is no conflict, and little need for a specialty writer's existence. Therefore every C-A-E-R-I subject should be examined carefully and thoroughly to discover the nature and degree to which a conflict may exist.

For example, one of the basic concepts in our democracy is that each person after a specified age is eligible to exercise the rights of a free citizen. Twenty-one years was the magic figure at which this maturity was acquired. However, in the last few years that age as a criterion for assuming certain responsibilities has been changed to help solve the problems, needs, feelings, and desires that existed. Today some contend that the new age laws have merely substituted one set of problems, needs, feelings, and desires for another.

The dichotomy that exists concerning this issue is similar to many that daily face the specialty writer. Similar conflicts exist about books, films, movies, and other aspects of our day-to-day existence.

Conflict is a normal part of human living. Therefore it should be used by the specialty writer to develop an identification with one or the other of each social, political, moral, or governmental concept he or she chooses to discuss. When conflict is not an obvious part of a situation, many imaginative and farsighted writers strongly imply its presence. In other words, every writer of a C-A-E-R-I must constantly keep in mind that some aspect of conflict is essential to the success of everything that is written.

Conflict is also a fundamental aspect of the next important attention factor, suspense.

Suspense as an Attention Factor

In a previous discussion of dramatic news it was said that suspense may be defined as the mental and emotional state of listener-viewer uncertainty about the end result or conclusion of what is being said, heard, or watched. Suspense, as a state of mental and emotional uncertainty about a conclusion or outcome, is inextricably linked with conflict. Where there is one of these elements, suspense or conflict, the other is never far away. That is why suspense is used as a story-telling technique by every successful writer. That is also why millions will, year after year, be enthusiastic about watching a national baseball or football play-off.

In a C-A-E-R-I, suspense is used to get the listener-viewer mentally and emotionally involved in what the specialty writer is talking about. As a result of this involvement, the listener-viewer should find it much easier to decide whose side to be on or which side to favor.

Once a listener-viewer is "hooked" by the suspense, the uncertainty involved in a conflict, an additional complication can be used to increase the suspense to the extent that the listener-viewer will be "hanging on" to the communicator's every word. Aristotle in the fourth century B.C. was the first to note the effectiveness of this aspect of oral-aural communicating we call suspense.[4]

USING THE ATTENTION FACTORS

Individuals frequently insist that they should be permitted to make up their own minds about civic issues and events. However, psychological studies show that human beings are not always "in total charge" of their ability to be objective. Human beings have the capacity to reason but there is a difference between capacity and achievement. Emotional bias is, in general, a human preference.[5]

Since Overstreet's study of this human characteristic, other psychological research studies have also shown that it is our emotions, feelings, and desires that determine our specific muscle tension, heart rate, worries, and irritabilities, rather than our ability to be reasonable, relaxed, and objective.[6] Therefore as a specialty writer for radio and television, keep in mind that all new, strange, or different points of view may be suspect to the majority of listener-viewers. The person whom you are attempting to help with your C-A-E-R-I may interpret your effort as a threat to his status quo, his well-being. Therefore as a writer you should avoid creating

[4] S. H. Butcher, trans., *Aristotle's Poetics* (New York: Hill and Wang, 1961).
[5] H. W. Overstreet, *The Mature Mind* (New York: W. W. Norton, 1949).
[6] Myer Friedman, M.D., and Ray H. Roseman, M.D., *Type A Behavior and Your Heart* (New York: Alfred A. Knopf, 1974).

extreme forms of anxiety in the listener-viewer because anxiety is an emotional response that fosters prejudice. And that prejudice is likely to be against you.

Prejudice in the listener-viewer may be alleviated by your being specific. When the writer is specific, the listener-viewer has a better chance to understand and is more likely to kinesthetically repeat what is being said. In other words, the listener-viewer will silently talk along with the communicator. On occasion the listener-viewer's lips will be moving. This is a form of empathic response.

A writer helps create this kind of listener-viewer response by being specific and by using attention factors that call up similar experiences. And because human beings depend on their personal frames of reference for understanding, the specialty writer should constantly remember that meanings are in people and not in the words to which they are listening.

MELODY AND RHYTHM IN SPECIALTY WRITING

The more melodic your written message is in an unaccented-accented pattern, the more speakable and meaningful your message is. When a message spoken aloud is understood and felt, its rhythm is said to help the listener-viewer identify with the thoughts and feelings being conveyed. Therefore, what is written to be spoken must be advantageously rhythmical and melodic. This means, in broadcasting, that the thought will be pleasing to the ear as well as logical to the mind.[7]

Technically, rhythmic regularity in what you write is identifiable by the alternation of one or more unaccented syllables combined with an accented syllable. The opening line of Lincoln's Gettysburg Address helps illustrate this phenomenon in prose.

> Four score and seven years ago, our fathers brought forth upon this continent a new nation conceived in liberty and dedicated to the proposition that all men are created equal.

Another example is the famous statement that can be found in Franklin D. Roosevelt's first inaugural address.

> The only thing we have to fear is fear itself.

Note how the rhythmic pattern helps the imagery and the emotional appeal turn these prose examples into language that is easily understood and remembered.

[7] John Diamond, M.D., *Behavioral Kinesiology* (New York: Harper and Row, 1979).

DEVELOPING A PROFESSIONAL ATTITUDE

A specialty writer must also understand certain communication techniques.

First, you need to understand vocal skills that are essential to communicating because you may be expected to do your own.

Second, you need to understand production skills and how these may be used to reinforce what is being communicated with the voice and on occasion with the body.

Third, you need to know what you can say and what must be left unsaid. As a specialty writer you do not have the right to communicate certain subject matter on radio or television. Neither do you have the freedom that makes it possible for other kinds of writers to "point a finger." You do not have this right because, as Chief Justice Warren Burger asserted, you cannot use public property, the air waves, for the purpose of advocating *unless what you say is in the public interest*. As a specialty writer, you must comply with the Communication Act of 1934, especially Section 315, the Fairness Doctrine.

In addition, you must know the limitations of the Federal Election Campaign Act, Section 31, of 1971. It too makes your writing life different from that of those who write for print. Furthermore, you must be aware that what you may say or may not say is often given additional restrictions by station policy.

Fourth, you must, as a specialty writer on the job, know firsthand all local business, civic, and governmental leaders. It is these individuals who make it possible for you as a writer to be considered capable of handling all sides of a controversial issue. Your non-partisan approach should indicate that you, as the station's representative, can be trusted to act fairly and justly in the interests of all concerned. Incidentally, many writers develop and keep that trust by being willing to go to jail rather than reveal the source of their information.

Treating all sources fairly is sometimes referred to as maintaining a balanced coverage. This means that you give everyone a reasonable opportunity to express a point of view concerning controversial issues. However, it does not mean that your station must furnish equal time for all those who are themselves controversial. Balanced coverage is a tight-rope you, as a professional, must learn to walk, even though it may take years of experience and practice.

GETTING READY TO WRITE

The amount of air-time available is the first thing you need to know when you are assigned to write a C-A-E-R-I. The number of seconds available determines how much you will write and your approach to the subject.

After the amount of time is settled you then begin to explore the subject matter.

There are many ways to locate information about a subject. However, the following fact-finder procedure generally produces a wide and useful variety of material for your fact sheet. These eight steps are:

1. *Subject.* Naturally you need to decide upon a topic and determine its thesis, theme, or central idea as it relates to a problem, need, feeling, or desire. Once this decision is made you proceed with the next step.

2. *Personal experiences.* Under this category you develop information by recalling and recounting experiences of your own as each relates to your topic. You will no doubt add to this step as you investigate the subject through interviews and other forms of questioning. Personal experience can make an important contribution to your data collection.

3. *Historical or biographical allusions.* Information that qualifies for an historical or biographical allusion should have a direct reference or relationship to your subject. The information you list under this category will show important relationships between your topic and an event or events in the past. Some of the information you collect for this step may be used as a causal reference.

4. *Statistical data.* The information collected under this category should be facts that have been developed through research. Such facts and statistics should relate to and/or help verify specific points you wish to make about your topic. The information listed here may be from laboratory observations, research experiments, reports made at meetings, or other forms of documentation.

5. *Reference to authority.* Under this step you include citations from authorities who, because of what they have said or believe, will support your point of view. These references may include authorities who have written books, journal articles, or reports, and are experts in the field of your topic.

6. *Causal relationships.* Under this step you place all the materials and information that can specifically be used to develop logical cause-to-effect points of view. A causal relationship between ideas or experiences implies or expresses a correlation between a cause and the effect it may create. Each fact that you develop should be linked to, or followed by, a specific effect.

7. *Analogies.* The term analogy implies that if two or more things agree with each other in some respect there will probably be an agreement in others. When two ideas or events have likenesses, that fact permits the writer to draw an analogy. List as many analogies as you can discover, or as many as you have evidence to support. The more you list the better, because some will prove to be more useful than others.

8. *Comparisons and contrasts.* You have already used this type of

information. You first met it when you began using the Seven-step Process. Contrast, you will recall, is the difference between two objects, ideas, concepts, or experiences. A contrast is made for the purpose of discovering specific differences. Differences are arrived at by placing things together so that dissimilarities may be pointed out. Comparisons are made between things, events, people, happenings, by bringing them together in order to point out likenesses.

These eight steps have, through use by other writers, been demonstrated to be exceptionally helpful in compiling background material for a C-A-E-R-I. Their use makes it possible to consider a subject from a broad perspective. Such a many-sided approach also gives the writer a chance to visualize and think objectively about a subject while getting ready to write.

TYPES OF SPECIALTY WRITING

Timeliness is the essence of specialty writing. You will be expected to write about what is happening or is about to happen as of a particular time or moment. Why taxes should or should not be raised. Why jail sentences are or are not adequate. Why one should or should not read such and such a book or see such and such a movie. Because you will be guided by the timeliness of an issue, examples for each of the following types of specialty writing are not given. Past events that prompted expressions of concern by specialty writers yesterday are dated. You can easily discover timely examples on all the networks and a few leading radio and television stations.

As you listen, note the correlation between what is said and the personality of the communicator.

Commentary

A commentary is a set of observations about a timely thesis, theme, or central idea that implies a problem, need, feeling, or desire. The thoughts expressed in the commentary are related to observations, annotations, or explanatory concepts. They are arranged together to illustrate your specific point of view. In this way the commentator and the commentary are inextricably linked. The person doing the commenting is usually considered to be an authority on the subject, and frequently is a "personality."

The original purpose of a commentary on radio or television was to give the commentator a chance to cover a number of items and to inject some personal views into one or more of the available news events. Today the commentator interprets or comments on any subject that seems important as of that moment. But nearly always what is said is from the commentator's personal point of view.

Most commentators relate what they talk about to some aspect of the "public weal." As a result, the commentator attracts attention not only by what he says, but by the way he says it. Saying it as only the commentator can say it is expected because the style relates to the writer's personality, mood, and even vocal characteristics. That is why listener-viewers like to listen to a commentator who is a personality. Most networks present one commentary on each long newscast.

Analysis

A well-prepared news program uses specific contrasts and balances in its overall structure. These contrasts are included to attract listener-viewer attention. The news analyst can provide these program contrasts by helping the listener-viewer focus attention and interest on what a news event means. Another way to develop listener-viewer interest in a news program is to have an analyst explain why an event occurred and why it is or is not important.

Through such contributions an analyst can create interest in the growth, change, and development of a concept for a community. On a day-to-day basis, what the analyst says can be an instrument that helps consolidate a coverage area.

For example, the listener-viewer of a news program should be helped to understand why a politician stays at home or makes trips abroad during a campaign. The listener-viewer should be helped to understand how high interest rates may relate to unemployment, or how unemployment may relate to inflation.

Regardless of the point of view presented, the news analyst remains objective during the presentation. The showmanship that characterizes some of the other C-A-E-R-Is should not be used. Each network usually presents a panel of analysts after each presidential address to the nation. Some leading stations have regular news analysts.

Editorial

The word editorial is a newspaper term. In the context of broadcasting it is something of a misnomer. Initially an editorial was an article in a newspaper or periodical in which the writer expressed the opinion of the publisher, editor, or editors. In broadcasting, an editorial is an organized statement that represents the opinion of the owner, manager, station, or broadcast channel.

The use of an editorial implies that the station is assuming a responsibility of leadership in its coverage area. Doing so means the station is expressing its desire to stand up and be counted. However, the majority of stations and channels are owned by corporations. Therefore management is an employee, not an owner, and like the others who work at the station, is not at liberty to editorialize in the name of the station. Corporate ownership tends to protect its investment by not getting involved in controversies. Management knows that every radio and television set has a dial for turning to other stations as well as an off button. Consequently when an editorial is presented, a disclaimer that the station alone is responsible for the opinions expressed usually precedes and follows the editorial.

The very nature of an editorial demands that the writer be sure of every fact used. Furthermore, showmanship must not accompany an editorial. While an editorial as a device for presenting an objective concept can be an important part of a station's service to a coverage area, at the same time the rights and privileges to do so may stir up too many questions about freedom of speech. That is why a station may avoid the editorial except on very special occasions.

Review

There is no one specific way that a book, a television film, or a movie should, as a creative contribution, be evaluated. A book that is held in high esteem as a literary masterpiece by some may be banned or given a public burning by others. Both the dictionary and the Bible have been given such treatment. Therefore any examination, consideration, or discussion of a book is primarily a matter of personal taste, opinion, or preference. The same is true of television movies or films. Because of this, those who write radio and television reviews tend to use a writing style and technique similar to the style used by individuals who write humorous commentaries.

Some suggest that the reason for writing reviews in the current style is that it is easier to be entertaining than it is to be objective. Others insist that commercial broadcasting is primarily entertainment and for a review to be otherwise would result in a lowering of the station's ratings. In other words, to interject humorless reviews into a program that is basically a series of entertainment features would be an indication of poor business judgment. The point is that entertainment seems to be taking precedence over commercial programming except on occasions when an incident demands a hard news presentation.

However, a review, whether it be of a book, a television film, or a movie, is a critical discussion based on a thorough examination and analysis of the content.

For some time now the two words criticism and review have been used interchangeably, particularly in reference to motion pictures and live theater. Today the word review, when referring to a literary work, implies a somewhat less formal analysis than does the word critique or criticism. Nonetheless, the term review is constantly used, whether it be for a movie, a play, or a book.

Even though radio and television are generally entertaining, and even though the person who writes reviews may be referred to as the television-movie critic, the product turned out by that writer is generally styled to fit three aspects of production-performance for popular broadcasting.

First, the review must describe the work in some detail.

Second, the reviewer must express a relevant and interesting opinion about the content and the nature of the product.

Third, the opinions expressed must be stated in an entertaining style and manner.

Listen to any movie or book review on one of the network programs. You may want to record one, see the movie, or read the book, and then compare what the reviewer says with your own reactions. This is a good exercise in developing an understanding of the current trends in reviewing for radio and television.

Interview

An interview is fundamentally a production. As a production it is a conversation or a formulated meeting during which one or more people question or consult with other individuals. While the interview as a genre is rapidly becoming a way of promoting products and services, it is also used as a device for presenting information.

As a production, an interview should not be scripted for broadcast presentation. It should, insofar as possible, be an extemporaneous performance and have about it certain elements that are called "show-biz." But regardless of whether the interview is for radio or television, it must be adequately prepared in advance of its presentation. This preparation is necessary even if the interviewee is not available for personal consultation.

The interviewer must be ready to ask logical, intelligent, and pertinent questions of the interviewee. To accomplish this, the interviewer should employ all the routine techniques used in preparing for each of the other C-A-E-R-Is.

Whether the interview is for radio or television, its success depends to a large extent on the interviewer's ability to get the interviewee to talk freely and fluently. Therefore, in preparing an interview, the interviewer must discover all that it is possible to know about the interviewee in relation to that person's expertise. This information frequently determines the thesis, theme, central idea, or point of view that will be followed in the interview. During this preparation period, if it is at all possible, some kind of initial talk with the interviewee should take place so you can become accustomed to the interviewee's way of thinking and physical mannerisms.

After you have completed the initial preparation, whether with or without the interviewee, you must develop an outline. This outline is based on the combined notes you have made from reading about the interviewee and the talk you have had with your guest. It is also helpful, when possible, to discuss the questions and the outline with the interviewee. Exceptions are when you deliberately plan to surprise the guest by asking unexpected questions, and, of course, when the guest is not available for preliminary questioning.

As you plan your questions be sure to arrange them in an ascending, not a descending, order of importance. The ascending order will allow you to use the principle of climax, as in the Five-step Process.

Under most circumstances each question is given a brief preliminary background build-up. This approach gives the interviewee a chance to think through his answer as you phrase the question. The procedure also gives the listener-viewer a chance to get ready to focus attention on the answer.

For a radio interview you should also work from an outline. On occasion you may find it helpful to condense the outline to a list of factual statements. It is from these statements that you will ad lib your questions.

It is never wise to script an interview. When you do, you tend to read the questions and the interviewee tends to sound as if he or she were reading the answers. The result is a dull presentation.

Summary

There is no preferred tactical approach to writing a specialty item. The basic problems in specialty writing have to do with how your listener-viewer reacts to what you say. Therefore you must write in a manner that will keep your story from being misinterpreted and misunderstood. Writing from "absolute facts" will not always protect you. And protection is necessary for you and the station. A libel suit is no joke. This means you must be ever alert to the possibility of being accused of libeling someone. The best way to do this is to understand the legal concepts of evidence.

While avoiding libel cannot always be assured even with the help of a good lawyer, you must always try. And even though you are speaking out intentionally for the public's good, that is not an adequate excuse. If you have not controlled your language sufficiently to avoid libel, you must be able and willing to prove in court that what you say is true. And even in today's courts, the truth is difficult to establish. Members of the CBS "60 Minutes" team face this problem constantly. Furthermore they readily admit that while they do everything they can to avoid making mistakes, nevertheless errors do occur.

The five types of specialty writing defined here can, each in its way, help you develop a feeling and a capacity for going beyond straight news reporting. Doing so can take you into that aspect of news reporting being developed by a few adventurous individuals who believe in social accountability. This credo states that everyone should be accountable for what he says and does. As a follower of this point of view you can go into in-depth reporting, interpretive reporting, investigative reporting, and documentary writing. Training in specialty writing is a beginning in this direction.

However, as you begin this aspect of your career you need to develop an even greater knowledge of broadcast law. For example, you must be certain that none of your statements are libelous or slanderous. You must be certain that what you say and how you say it invades no one's privacy. And above all, you must never violate any of the rules laid down by the Federal Communication Commission, the Federal Trade Commission, or other rule-making agencies. You must constantly keep in mind that as a newswriter you are accountable for what you write. Therefore, you must know how to check and double-check before releasing what you say.

Being aware of the legal aspects of evidence does help. But always before you respond to any accusation, you must talk with management. This is essential because being accused of libel is like being in a car accident. You are not the best witness to what happened. Therefore be sure to study carefully the suggestions under libel in your United Press International *Stylebook*.[8]

ASSIGNMENTS

It is assumed that before you begin writing a C-A-E-R-I you will have become adept at writing news.

1. To get experience writing a commentary, select a series of newspaper stories about the same news event. Based on the information in these stories use the eight steps of the fact finder to help you organize information with the aim of developing a fact sheet. Let the subject matter determine whether you develop it by following the Six-, Seven-, or Five-step Process.

2. You will find it helpful to use one of the processes or a combination of the steps. Under the appropriate step of the process you are

[8] United Press International, *Stylebook* (New York: 1981).

following, place the appropriate information you have from your fact sheet. For example, suppose you decide to write your commentary using the Seven-step Process. In all probability you will need a page for each step. Therefore, on page one you list all the information that will help you write the Step 1 statement, a thesis, theme, or central idea as it relates to a problem, need, feeling, or desire that is suggested by the total data available to you.

3. On page two you list the data that will supply the information you need for Step 2. This information will help you repeat the initial statement in different words.

4. On page three you list all the information from your fact sheet that will help you write Step 3. These will be details and examples to illustrate Step 1.

5. Continue following this procedure for Steps 4, 5, 6, and 7, unless you decide you do not need one or more of these steps.

6. Then go back to Step 1, page one, and write your lead statement. When you have it ready, you then write Step 2.

7. Step 3 will need details. It has been found helpful to write Step 3 as if it were a total process. For example, you may write Step 3 as a Six-step Process, or your information may dictate that you write Step 3 as a modified Seven-step Process.

8. The important thing to keep in mind is that whenever you write a paragraph, it is to your advantage to develop it in terms of either six or seven steps. This is the very essence of composing, putting a thought together. Always when you need help in stimulating your *intuition*, use a process to help you get going.

When you have finished writing a rough draft of your commentary, revise it.[9] Always use the guide at the end of this chapter during this procedure.

9. List ten analysis topics that you believe apply to your local radio or television coverage area. Use the fact finder to help you develop a fact sheet. Then collect your information and write two ninety-second analyses. Always when you have finished writing use the revision guide for checking what you have said.

10. If there is time, develop two editorials based on the previously collected news stories. Follow the same procedure used in the two previous assignments for writing each.

11. Select a movie and a book to review. Use the fact finder for planning and any one of the writing processes you prefer for writing a ninety-second review of each.

---

[9] Writing several commentaries and using different processes or combinations of each is an excellent way to perfect your writing technique and to develop your intuition and personal style.

12. Prepare a two-minute interview for broadcasting by using the author of an article in a professional journal as the interviewee and the information in the article as the source for the interviewee's answers. Remember, this is a make-believe interview. It is done for the purpose of giving you experience in working with questions and answers. Do not go to see the author even though he or she may be available on your campus. Your questions and the answers for them should come from the journal article.

Write out the interviewee's answers to your proposed questions. Your instructor may want another person to serve as the interviewee to give you experience in forming questions extemporaneously.

Your instructor may want to omit the interviewing routine or even have you do it live on tape. These routines are fun, but they take time away from writing. Production of this kind can always come later.

Each time you finish writing a commentary, analysis, editorial, review, or the questions for an interview, be sure to check what you have written with the following guide. Then rewrite as the need indicates, and in terms of the process you followed. The best way to edit your copy is to be objective. Treat it as if it belonged to another person and your job is to improve it.

A GUIDE TO REVISING

- Have you used words with specific meanings? If not, have you qualified these words?
- Did you use active, not passive voice?
- Did you make each sentence as short as possible?
- Did you limit each sentence to one thought?
- Did you leave out all words and ideas that are not relevant?
- Did you check the melody of your language and when and where you needed to change the accent to make it more dynamic?
- Does what you have written fulfill the function and purpose of each step in the process you followed?

FINAL SUGGESTIONS FOR WRITING

Now that the use of the processes has become a conscious part of your writing effort, approach each assignment intuitively. Writing intuitively means letting your developed ability to communicate take over. Naturally you will use all the help you can get in collecting data and in making notes to develop a fact sheet. But in terms of writing, if you have by now had enough experience, you may be able to sit down and write without having to think step by step through what you are going to say and how you are going to say it. But don't be disappointed if it takes additional experience to help you achieve this status. Many writers struggle through every word. But they write.

When you have written an assignment intuitively, read it and make such changes as are necessary. In making these changes you may want to use the processes to help you. All professional writers use some such device. Why shouldn't you? After all, the ability to be logical and objective is the professional writer's ace in the hole.

Glossary of Broadcast News Terms

AP Associated Press. This is one of the major news services in the United States. It is a cooperative service owned by its members.

A-Wire A primary wire service offered to newspapers by the two major news services, the Associated Press and the United Press International. All A-Wire copy is written in newspaper style. Its stories cover primarily national and international news.

actuality A taped or live interview or a news event that is used in a radio newscast.

air talent Any person who performs regularly before a radio microphone or a television camera.

anchor person The number-one personality on a newscast.

assignment editor The person responsible for assigning and checking the day's news coverage events. Television stations and large radio stations usually have such a person.

audio Sound on radio and on television.

B-Wire   A secondary wire service prepared by the Associated Press and United Press International for newspapers. The B-Wire service is written in newspaper style and consists of less important news such as feature stories, full texts of speeches, reports, and leftovers from the A-Wire service.

backtiming   A timing procedure used in all types of broadcasting. In news, it is the technique of timing the last two or three stories so the newscaster will know whether to speed up, slow down, cut, or pad as he approaches the end of the newscast, which must finish exactly on time.

beat   A routine news assignment covered regularly by a reporter. These assignments may be handled in person, by telephone inquiry, or both.

billboard   A succinct announcement on the air that a certain advertiser is sponsoring a portion of a program or newscast.

bridge   The unit in a newscast that is the link between two sound video tapes or film segments, or between silent and sound. It is read or spoken by the newscaster. The bridge may be done on location and edited into a story later.

bulletin   A program-breaking story. It is one paragraph in length and is sent double spaced over the wire so it may be communicated immediately. Updating and other details of these stories are sent on the news wire as details become available.

chromakey   An electronic process for combining two or more television pictures. Current use in newscasting combines moving video or a slide with headlines behind the anchor person.

commercial   An advertisement broadcast on radio or television.

copy   A completed news story. Also used in referring to the script of a broadcast commercial.

cover shot   A wide-angle film or camera shot showing the entire scene.

cut   In news a specific section of film, videotape, or audiotape that is selected for a news story. Also a change from one picture to another.

cutaway   A film shot technique in news wherein the camera moves from the main feature to a related one. A technique for continuing a dramatic scene without overdoing it. A camera shot going from the victim's body to his hat nearby is an example.

dateline   The geographic location of a news story.

director   The person in charge of the studio and control room while the newscast is in progress.

drive time   Those hours of the day when large segments of the population are driving cars to and from work, and may be listening to car radios.

E C U   (extreme close-up) Used in news to frame the eyes, nose, and mouth of a person being interviewed. The rest of the face may be cropped by the camera.

E J   Electronic journalism. Sometimes used for **E N G**.

E N G   (electronic news gathering) Use of a portable videotape recorder. The tape, or line picture and sound, may be beamed back to the station via microwave for immediate airing or editing.

fill copy or **filler**   The extra news copy taken along with the planned news, just in case the newscaster runs short and padding (filler) is needed.

flash   A priority news service story of three to six words sent only by national desks. It probably should be broadcast immediately. Always ask your station about priority.

flip card   The same technical arrangement as a studio card. It is a still graphic used in special news stories.

free-lance or **free-lancer**   A self-employed individual who sells stories, photos, or news stories to television and radio stations.

freeze frame   A single frame used in a film as a still visual.

future book or **file**   An information file detailing all future news events and their dates.

handout   Refers to a public relations film or news release. These are sent free by publicity seekers to radio and television stations and other news media.

hard news   A news story that stresses news values instead of human interest or humor. Most short newscasts are made up of hard news.

kicker   A humorous or human interest story placed last in a newscast to give the program a lift.

lead   The opening statement of a news story whose purpose is to introduce the listener-viewer to an H-O-E-O.

lead-in   Copy that introduces an audiotape, sound film, or V T R.

lead-out   A sentence or two that is read by the newscaster after the audiotape or sound film for the purpose of reestablishing the identity of the person talking.

library film News film that is filed for reuse in the event the particular story breaks again.

live opener The live introductory portion of a sound film story.

localize The process of rewriting an international, national, or regional news story so that it will be more relevant because of the local angle or slant the writer gives it.

N.A.B. The abbreviation for The National Association of Broadcasters.

news director The administrator in the radio or the television news department.

out takes or **cuts** Those sections of film or tape that are not used after a news story has been edited.

producer The person in charge of the news program production.

promo A promotional announcement for the station.

P S A A public service announcement.

R.T.N.D.A. Radio Television News Directors Association.

sequence A series of film or videotape shots that follows a chronological order.

shot A continuous run of film or videotape from the time the camera is turned on until it stops when the camera angle or direction is changed.

shot sheet A listing on paper of all the shots taken by the photographer for a specific news story.

SIL An abbreviation for silent film.

slug The identifying information that is usually placed in the upper right-hand corner of the news script. Placement may vary from station to station. This information includes the writer's name, date, and a brief description of the story.

SOF An abbreviation for sound on film.

spot A term used instead of the term commercial.

standup The news person who is seen speaking at the scene in a film or live report.

stringer An individual who works for a station, not on a full time basis, but who is paid for each news item.

SYNC (pronounced "sink") A short term for synchronization. The term is used in news when referring to the coordination of the film and the sound.

tag line Similar to a lead-out. It reestablishes the identity of the person(s) in the report(s).

talent A term used to refer to an individual who regularly appears on radio or television, especially in commercials.

tape line-up A list of the news film, arranged in the order of its presentation.

tease or **teaser** A brief statement designed to promote news stories or reports that will be given later in the newscast. Its purpose is to create interest and keep the listener-viewer tuned to the station.

update The latest development available about a news story.

UPI United Press International. One of the two major news services in the United States. It is a stock company specializing in selling news to the news media.

V-O (voice-over) The script portion of a news story that is read aloud during a film or videotape presentation.

V T R Videotape recorder, or a recording.

voicer Any audiotape news report made by a news person.

Index

Kipling, Rudyard, 40

Repetition, 42
  purposeful redundancy, 43
  as reinforcement, 49
Reporting
  advocacy, 2–3
Review, writing of, 133–134
Revision guide, 138
Roosevelt, Franklin D., 128

Said, use of, 23–26
Satisfaction statement, 49
Seven-step TV news script
  example, 72–73
Shalit, Gene, 124
Shannon, Claude E., 1
Single-meaning words, 97–100
Six-step process examples, 53–55
Soft news lead, 55–58
Specialty writing
  attention factors, 125–128
Specificity, 23
  synonyms, use of, 23–26
Statistics in news, 33–35
Style, 84–100, 101–122
Suspense in news, 73, 74
Synonyms, 98–100

Television news, 13–14
  attribution, 29–31
  copy type size, 14
  format, 15
  radio, differences from, 13–15
  story lengths, 14
  with videotape, 70–73
Tense, 18–22
  future, 19
  future perfect, 19
  past, 19
  past perfect, 19
  present, 18–19
  present perfect, 19
That, use of, 93
Titles, 27
  in leads, 27
  in stories, 27–31
To, too, two, use of, 88
Transitional words and phrases
  external, 117–122

  function, 101–102
  internal, 102–116
Turner Broadcasting System, 8

United Press International,
  Stylebook, 37

Visualization, 49
Voice, 22–23
Voicers, 14

Weaver, Warren, 1
Which, use of, 93
Word usage, 84–100
  compared to, 92
  compared with, 92
  contractions, 88–89
  multimeaning, 98–100
  name calling, 94–96
  pronoun reference, 89
  redundancies, 91
  single meanings, 97–98
  synonyms, 98–100
  that and which, 93
  verbs (was and were), 91
  wordiness, 88
Writing
  analysis, 132
  commentary, 131
  editorial, 132
  encoding, 4–5
  human interest, 80–82
  review, 133
  sports, 78–80
  techniques, 101–122
  words, use of, 84–100
Writing news, 46–82
  five-step, 75–78
  initial statement, 48–50
  process approach, 46–47
  seven-step, 75–78
  six-step, 60–65
Writing problems
  immediacy, 18
  specificity, 23–26
  tense, 18–22
  voice, 22–23